Social Medi
Beg

*Step-By-Step Guide to Social Media
Advertising. Learn From Best Practices and
Grow Your Business*

By Alex Douglas

The information provided herein is stated to be truthful and consistent, in that any liability, in terms of inattention or otherwise, by any usage or abuse of any policies, processes, or directions contained within is the solitary and utter responsibility of the recipient reader. Under no circumstances will any legal responsibility or blame be held against the publisher for any reparation, damages, or monetary loss due to the information herein, either directly or indirectly.

Respective authors own all copyrights not held by the publisher.

The information herein is offered for informational purposes solely and is universal as so. The presentation of the information is without contract or any type of guarantee assurance.

The trademarks that are used are without any consent, and the publication of the trademark is without permission or backing by the trademark owner. All trademarks and brands within this book are for clarifying purposes only and are the owned by the owners themselves, not affiliated with this document.

Table of contents

Introduction:

Welcome to the new technologies!

Introduction to SMM

The primary purpose of writing this book is to provide people with a complete guide preamble to Social Media Marketing to the scholars. This introduction can't wait for the understudies everything, and it's also for the delegate who could be working in any affiliation. The convergence of this book resolves to offer a compact introduction and, therefore, the fundamental utilization of Social Media Marketing. It's the place all the eager people that got to learn SMM get information about the use and odds of Social Media Marketing.

As I allow you to know round the start, this book wants to add up of the way to help people with starting to do Social Media promoting within the road, which has an enormous amount of fun, and that they need to get capacities. This book wants to assist people with learning internet organizing, advancing, and obtain money from different techniques like re-appropriating work, helpful exertion, impermanent position work, or another quite work.

The purpose of writing this book is to provide you with a complete sense of SMM. How to do it? What are the main parts of SMM? Why we do and the importance of SMM. Nowadays, SMM is essential for people who want to work with new technologies.

The truth is, online life publicizing has various choices, particularly within the "gadgets" area, and it's developed quickly. That gathers there is a colossal measure of fabric out there. It'll generally be overpowering! Notwithstanding, it can comparably be through, and thru possible just in case you allow compromising within the development, make steady advances, give things an attempt, and assembling your sureness.

For instance, I had a mate who wants to be a writer. He was checking out new position openings, so I kicked him off in online life. "There are such a significant number of contraptions out there, "he wants to state," How I'm ever getting to get settled with all of them?"

The correct response is that you simply do not have to urge the ability with all of them. Nobody can. I pushed my accomplice to not stress over trying to push the hang of everything, besides to a point to urge to understand the wanderer pieces during a manner of speaking.

My mate worked in Facebook progressing, took in genuinely about Twitter, and found out to locate an area affiliation that gave him a made shots at performing some free web-based all-consuming purpose. The calling didn't just bring him; he expected to put essentialness into it.

Following a couple of years after the fact, the individual doing full-time outsourcing work in Social Media Marketing and making Google promotions.

This book used to associate with the centre zones of computerized promoting, content, Ad Words, social, and investigation (CASA for short). The fundamental objective of composing this book is to strengthen how every one of these zones is associated. Advertisement Words is a device for Google. It used to make promotions for web index showcasing. The inspiration for composing this book originated from my expert foundation, just as research about the new commercial centre and 22nd-century advancements.

A year ago, in January 2016, there were 3.5 billion web clients on the planet, which is 46% of the total populace. Of that populace, there were 2.3 billion of those clients who were dynamic online networking account clients.

Internet-based life can't utilize to make an offer substance while associating with loved ones; it is currently additionally being used to showcase in the business world, which is known as web-based social networking promoting. Web-based social networking advertising characterizes as, "The utilization of internet-based life sites and informal communities to showcase an organization's items and administrations. Web-based social networking showcasing furnishes organizations with an approach to arrive at new clients and draw in with existing clients". Online networking is turning into a ground-breaking intensifying impact; be that as it may, it is a dubious issue with regards to business. The problem that lies here is if organizations/organizations should utilize online networking to advertise. Many accept organizations should remain off internet-based life destinations since it causes difficulties and dangers. A case of these difficulties and risks are time the executives and the negative informal. Be that as it may, there are approaches to defeat this. Then again of this issue, internet-based life is turning into a groundbreaking issue for organizations, and it ought to exploit. It is an essential instrument for showcasing because it takes into consideration a full scope of ad, with it being the most financially savvy approach to arrive at mass measures of clients. Online life is turning into the better plan to advertise and turning into the distinction showcase in organizations; it is making way for new chances, purchaser cooperation's, and experiences, and has promoting viability and thus, this is the reason internet based life advertising is a smart thought for organizations.

Making way for new open doors is one of the numerous advantages that web-based life advertising has. An examination done said 57% of small and medium-sized undertakings (SMEs) said internet-based life was useful to their business. The advantages took into consideration SMEs to be productive by the new changes, and those are brand presentation, expanded objective traffic, drives age, and market experiences.

SMM takes place when someone wants to introduce their new product in the market. That how the person should design the product. How effectively the product organizes. The person who wants to learn SMM of the product convinces the buyer with his expertise and takes his product and increases the sale of the product by doing the SMM.

At that point, along these lines, it considers the capacity to accumulate information on the client, for example, age, sexual orientation, topographical area, interests.

This data finds organizations to target clients dependent on these elements explicitly. It was account for that expanding traffic was the following significant advantage in 2016, with a 75% positive outcome. Next, there is drive age, which is potential clients or deals possibilities. Many clients are via web-based networking media, which takes into consideration the odds of producing new clients. 66% of organizations found that drives age improved their raggedness in 2016. Ultimately, showcase bits of knowledge consider the information that left in the file of online life locales to utilize for data; for example, target crowds and the contenders are made open. Then again, of this, it additionally takes into consideration the chance to keep an eye on your rivals' since you can watch and read what is occurring on their sites, online journals, and web-based life destinations. Picking up of market bits of knowledge was likewise seen as 66% valuable to organizations.

These four new open doors that are made through online networking show how compelling they can be for organizations.

This proof demonstrates how online networking promoting is useful for organizations and ought to exploit.

This take is as meagre as six hours of the week to begin seeing these outcomes. Organizations will see these chances if they simply contribute their endeavours with web-based life for six hours or less.

The aftereffects of these endeavours similarly as meagre as six hours or less expanded all territories. The expansion right now 92% business introduction, 79% traffic increment, 66% leads to age, and 63% market knowledge. Everything necessary to begin getting results from internet-based life openings is only six hours per week or less, and it will keep on expanding.

Client cooperation and bits of knowledge are other additional advantages of online networking showcasing.

Client communications consider current clients and potential clients to interface with the business by leaving remarks, input, and suppositions.

With online life locales, these clients can leave criticism and offer their feelings, yet they can likewise demand help and backing on the off chance that it is required. By having this capacity of correspondence, it improves the connection among buyers and organizations.

It considers an increasingly close to home and subjective treatment for the item and administration they have bought. Interfacing organizations to purchasers create connections and help conveniently cultivate them. Having the option to draw in and connect with potential and current purchasers supports that expanded feeling of closeness of this client relationship. Having these connections are necessary for the present business condition since unwavering shopper ness can disappear at the littlest misstep. Organizations endeavour on the expression of their faithful clients; it is significant.

Shoppers who have had a decent online networking administration involvement in a brand they are 71% bound to prescribe it to other people. These excellent internet-based life administration helps manufacture stable fan bases and the positive informal. Organizations saw a 68% expansion in their dependable fan base because of online networking advertising.

With having an internet-based life accessible, it has the component of its promptness.

How this done is when, for example, if your business chooses to utilize Facebook as one of their online life decisions.

The minute when a client/potential client makes an audit, remarks, post, or notices your business, your administrator will get a warning to make a move on this. It takes into consideration opportune reactions and for a client to talk legitimately with somebody. Clients need to be reacted to immediately and not pause, and mainly not get any nonexclusive mechanized opinions. Everything considers a business to give their clients a fantastic encounter, and like this builds up a dependable fan base. It shows how successful internet-based life showcasing can be for organizations, and how this is a smart thought to put resources into online life promoting.

Advertising adequacy is about cost-effectiveness since it considers organizations to make a showcasing nearness and advance their image while setting aside cash and time. It is such a successful showcasing device since it needn't bother with high publicizing costs or even high measures of time.

Most online life locales are free, which takes into consideration organizations to do this without paying to utilize these destinations, or for those that do charge, it is generally modest.

It considers it to cost putting something aside for organizations because there are no high publicizing costs. Being financially savvy is such a preferred position since you can see the more noteworthy rate of return that holds a more excellent spending plan for other advertising and operational expense. As per an examination done, the more significant part of the individuals who go through in any event 11 hours out of each week via web-based networking media endeavours saw an advantage of decreased advertising costs. Another examination recommended that 96% of entrepreneurs/advertisers utilize web-based life showcasing, and 92% of those concur or emphatically concur with the expression that, "Web-based life promoting is significant for my business." With web-based life, the word spreads at a lot quicker pace. Various clients who utilize web-based presence and have individuals that like, remark, and offer with their companions on the system, make for conveying content simpler. Indeed, even with that, the substance goes onto web crawlers, which brings more guests and conceivably new clients, it is an incredible cycle.

Indeed, even merely beginning with web-based life advertising, for apprentices that have under twelve hours of experience and just went through less than five hours out of each week observed a 54% advantage to their business. Half of the organizations who depend via web-based networking media promoting saw a half-diminished showcasing cost for their business. These examinations all lead to the point that online networking advertising carries adequacy to organizations while permitting them to make a nearness and advance themselves while setting aside cash and time. Organizations need to have the option to set aside themselves time and money, and with online life advertising, they can do this along these lines indicating how web-based life showcasing is a smart thought.

Numerous organizations stress over time the board with regards to online life showcasing. The stress is that there may be more than one representative, some of the time, even a gathering of workers that should be prepared to speak with clients and react to their criticism and grumblings on every day.

They additionally may need a worker or representatives that are exceptionally gifted and prepared in online life, promoting to do this successfully.

Representatives should have the option to focus via web-based networking media advertising since it very well may be tedious. In addition to the fact that they need to have the opportunity to submit, they additionally must be dynamic and produce new substances usually to remain on the radar and be successful. It is a worry for those entering internet-based life promoting.

Time the board is an issue that can survive. Organizations can devote as much time as they might want to their web-based life systems. Studies have demonstrated, as I have examined as of now, that it just takes six hours or less every week to begin getting results. Six hours or less is the whole week by week time responsibility for web-based life advertising. A critical 63% of advertisers are utilizing online networking for six hours and have seen this as the best time.

The best answer for the time the executives is to have a successful administration plan.

The ten hints that recommend for viability are: have an arrangement, don't stress over flawlessness, centre around each apparatus in turn, show up reliably, utilize your voice on the web, set a period limit, turn off notices, plan new substance posts, audit investigation, and set a healthy profit for your venture.

Time the executives can survive, so it shouldn't hold up traffic for organizations to get on board with web-based social networking promoting because it is a smart thought for organizations.

Unfavourable, informal exchange is likewise a factor business consider before entering the market. A client can leave negative surveys, remarks, and appraisals since they might be unsatisfied, and it can promptly go to the internet-based life page for others to see. It can hazard a business's notoriety.

What the entirety of the different web-based life pages share for all intents and purpose are that they empower discussion, it makes the verbal. Organizations can't control the debate through internet-based life; be that as it may, they can endeavour to impact it utilizing gatherings.

On the off chance that advertisers can use the internet-based experience to be confident, it very well may be a gainful apparatus.

Research has been done and analyzes how organizations can manage negative customer informal and transform it into a positive way. These five methodologies are: delay, react, accomplice, legitimate activity, and control.

The defer procedure is the possibility that if an organization defers the reaction of the harmful online life crusade, that it will fade away all alone in trusts, the organization doesn't need to react or disregard the client protest out and out. This procedure just permits time for the organization to survey the rally so they can build up a careful reaction to the issue. Postponing a contrary assault keeps the organization from taking part in a "back-and-forth" contest. The subsequent procedure is to react. By reacting, it includes tuning in to, recognizing, and possibly tending to the negative input that creates. Organizations can utilize this technique to contact clients and tune in to their protests to help give a positive encounter so clients can feel they have remained caught, and their issues were motivated on the way in the direction of a particular plane. The third is the accomplice, which is one of relationship or affiliation. This thing uses to join the outer side of the world. Another system is a lawful activity which includes one gathering starting a legal continuing against another; be that as it may, this restricts legitimate activities concerning web-based life. It is a technique that occasionally utilized because be that as it may, it is there if need be.

In conclusion, there is control, and this is expelling or stifling undesirable data via web-based networking media. Oversight is shielding the organization's brand pictures from harmful assaults. These methodologies take into consideration organizations to read if they experience negative verbal, which, if they do, they can make it head-on. Being set up for this considers organizations to have the option to utilize web-based life advertising since it benefits them.

Albeit web-based life showcasing can be a dubious issue, the positives exceed the negatives. Online networking advertising is a smart thought for organizations, which has been appeared all through this paper. Time the executives and unfavourable verbal exchange can be overwhelmed with the right administration plan, responsibility, and procedures. 3.8 million people in the U.S. have said that their buying choices are affected by web-based life. It demonstrates the amount of an effect internet-based life can play in the realm of advertising.

The effect web-based life advertising can bring to a business can be sure and advantageous.

Internet-based life has been a wonder that has just changed an enormous part of how organizations showcase in light of the positive effects, for example, new chances, buyer collaborations, and bits of knowledge, and promoting adequacy, which at last backings the contention that web-based life advertising is to be sure a smart thought.

Core Areas of Digital Marketing:

- **Content/ SEO:**
- o Content and SEO go connected at the hip. Without one, your endeavours, on the other, genuinely decreased. For instance, your catchphrase won't do much good except if you, at that point, utilize those watchwords in your substance. What's more, making content without realizing what your crowd is searching for will leave you with no critical traffic. Past that, an excellent substance is a thing that wins you backlinks, and its likewise what web indexes creep when they show up at your webpage.
- **Ad Words:**
- o It is the process of creating and managing ads on Google (Ad Word). It is the place where you get the people who click on your ads by the search for some keywords in Google. You pay when someone clicks on your ad.

- **Social Media Marketing:**
  - SMM is the process of creating products more accessible. Nowadays, SMM is essential because of marketplace competition.
  - This book is a manual that shows how to do SMM from different websites.
- **Analytics (Web Visitors):**
  - To quantify the presence of a web site, consultants and advertisers see Website traffic: the complete range of site guest's aboard information on wherever they originated from and the way they got from that time to the positioning.
  - Understanding the concept of traffic, a way to build the number of guests, a way to amendment over traffic into shoppers, and why traffic is lower on Saturday nighttime's is that the method into your on-line thriving.

Why we use Social Media Marketing

For some cutting-edge businesspeople, the enormous showcasing thing nowadays is web-based life. For a few, it's only a transitory yet the ground-breaking business craze or, on the other hand, a pattern that each businessperson and advertising proficient must exploit while still hot. In any case, to other people, it's only a well-known word that offers no handy advantage and can be an extremely muddled and soak expectation to learn and adapt.

Online life has, by one way, or another earned notoriety with specific individuals as just being a passing promoting prevailing fashion or pattern and all things considered, one that is unfruitful only because it showed up rather rapidly. Scarcely any organizations are enlivened to work through learning another and some of the time testing framework when the more established techniques appear to be dependable, particularly if they don't anticipate that such a strategy should be practical. They see it as an insignificant blip on a few people's radars as it were. Be that as it may, measurements tend to offer an alternate interpretation of it, an altogether different one. Well, known inbound promoting programming stage HubSpot noticed that in 2014, 92% of advertising experts said that online life showcasing played a significant job in their organizations with as much as 80% of them asserting that their sites' traffic went up as a result of it. Online networking Examiner – a United States-based media organization, said that 97% of showcasing experts use internet-based life advertising, albeit 85% of those they reviewed conceded not knowing which internet-based life apparatuses the best ones are to utilize.

Unmistakably, this shows web-based social networking showcasing has incredible potential for jacking up deals, yet then again, the capacity to utilize it ideally for accomplishing such results is yet ailing when all said in done. In case you're commonly confused concerning how you can use online life promoting furthering your business' potential benefit, here's a rundown of that can assist you with getting comfortable with the advantages your company may appreciate from utilizing this sort of promoting movement.

Better Trend Awareness

Consider each opportunity you get how to expand your business' permeability, and the syndicated content is entirely significant. What's more, outstanding amongst other better approaches to feature your business' substance receipt is through your internet-based life systems. Utilizing them can make your business increasingly open and more straightforward to contact, making it increasingly unmistakable and recognizable to your current, just as forthcoming clients.

A genuine case of this is a regular client of Twitter, who gets some answers concerning your business and its items or administrations directly after the individual in question discovered it in his or then again, her Twitter news channel.

Another genuine model would be a something else aloof potential client who may turn out to be increasingly acquainted with your item or then again administration only after the individual sees it on different informal organizations. In these manners, web-based life can permit you to pull in an unquestionably progressively across the board client base as it empowers you to get your business out there on the social feeds of your latent capacity demographic, even the ones that would have been trying to focus without this innovation. By observing your image showing up as they peruse through Twitter or by seeing that a portion of their companions loved you on Facebook, you are drawing in an ever-increasing number of individuals to your business, eventually bringing about more deals for your business.

Higher customer Loyalty

A distributed report by Texas Tech University noticed that organizations that online utilization networking to draw in clients to appreciate more devotion from them contrasted with the individuals who don't.

The report decides that organizations must make full utilize of accessible web-based life instruments to interface with their crowd.

An open and critical web-based life plan can be enormously valuable as far as improving clients' image reliability. In another examination, this time by Convince & Convert, announced that about 53% of Americans who are adherents of specific brands in web-based social networking would, in general, be increasingly faithful to such brands contrasted with the individuals who don't. The consequence of these examinations likely is connected to the way that internet-based life can target clients closer to home level than every single past type of publicizing. It empowers you to request an accessible assessment utilizing surveys, games, and other enjoyment and drawing in exercises that pull in clients to your business and afterwards keep up their consideration. The way cultivates that online networking permits your customers to feel like they have a job in forming your business, your items, your techniques they feel esteemed, and critical to the procedures your business goes through. They become faithful to the organizations that empower them to experience such positive sentiments.

More conversion opportunities

At whatever point you post something on your business' web-based life pages, you give a chance to your business to persuade its crowd to play out a specific activity, which is classified "transformation."

When you construct your business' following, you promptly access a wide range of clients - old ones, ongoing ones, and new ones. Further, you get the chance to draw in or connect with them. Each remark, video, blog entry, or picture that you share on your business' internet-based life pages offers individuals the chance to respond, and these responses can conceivably lead them to visit your site – potential transformations. Simply remember that not all collaborations with your business direct to changes, however, that each and each positive connection raises the odds of a genuine difference. Any positive response is probably going to bring issues to light, and the more mindfulness raised, the more prominent the probability of picking upshifts. Web-based life advertising is achieved, to some extent, through verbal. The more magnificent quality posts and substance you share, the more your companions and supporters like, top choice, or offer it, and the more mindfulness and enthusiasm for your organization spreads. On the off chance that your business' site experiences low navigate rates, the gigantic sum of possibilities accessible via web-based networking media can end up being particularly useful.

Furthermore, on the off chance that you'd prefer to get an opportunity of transformation, the first and generally significant things you need are open doors for such

Higher rates for the conversion

In a few manners, internet-based life showcasing can prompt a higher pace of change for your business' sites. Conceivably the most critical way it does so is through an "acculturation impact," i.e., it makes your business more like an individual rather than a, well, business.

Web-based life gives organizations chances to act and act as though they're individuals, which is significant because reality individuals typically favour working with individuals and not merely with inert foundations. It has additionally appeared in contemplates that online networking has a whole lot higher lead-to-close rate, which is the level of deals drives that, in the end, purchase an organization's items or administrations, contrasted with outbound promoting.

Clients are increasingly disposed to confide in a business that falls off an amiable and amiable like somebody they could be companions with, rather than mostly a chilly, withdrew establishment.

Getting the chance to draw in with your business in a way that feels cosy to your customer base can pick up their trust and conviction, and the specialized techniques web-based life offers can empower you to achieve precisely that.

Having a ton of web-based social networking devotees can likewise improve your business' trust and believability with clients a type of material evidence. A great many people are, to a few degrees, adherents. If their companions or those they follow are a piece of your client base, new clients are undeniably increasingly slanted to esteem your business liable to be a decent one deserving of their help. Along these lines, it makes a ton of sense to utilize web-based life to make critical upgrades in your business sites' present transformation rates.

Brand Authority

At the point when you consistently cooperate with your clients, you demonstrate transparency to other forthcoming clients.

At the point when clients need to boast about or supplement your administration or item, they'll most presumably go to the Internet and, specifically, web-based life.

Furthermore, when they post about your administration or issue, the odds are that new crowds or potential clients might need to follow your item or administration brand via web-based networking media for additional updates. Your item or administration will begin to turn out to be progressively essential and definitive again; individuals talk about it over web-based life. Likewise, your item or administration's scope and noticeable power can altogether improve on the off chance that you similarly communicate with a portion of the significant players in your industry on Facebook, Twitter, or other famous online life locales. Agreeable chitchat, with both your clients and your rivals, awards you a progressively all around created human face for your business, empowering you to venture a social picture that your clients and potential clients will come to trust and appreciate.

Lower cost of marketing products and services

At the point when you usually associate with your clients, you demonstrate honest intentions to other imminent clients.

At the point when clients need to gloat about or supplement your administration or item, they'll most likely go to the Internet and specifically, web-based life.

What's more, when they post about your administration or topic, the odds are that new crowds or potential clients might need to follow your item or administration brand via web-based networking media for additional updates. Your question or administration will begin to turn out to be increasingly essential and definitive again, and individuals talk about it over internet-based life. Likewise, your item or administration's span and obvious position can fundamentally improve on the off chance that you similarly communicate with a portion of the significant players in your industry on Facebook, Twitter, or other well-known online life locales. Agreeable talk, with both your clients and your rivals, awards you a progressively all around created human face for your business, empowering you to venture a social picture that your clients and potential clients will come to trust and appreciate.

Better experience for customers

Internet-based life is fundamentally a specialized apparatus naturally, much like telephone calls or messages. Each time you cooperate with a client via web-based networking media, you have the chance to advance your associations with your present and existing clients by openly exhibiting the elevated level of your client support, what's more, giving them extraordinary encounters.

It can be undeniable in the manner you handle protests about your item or administration on Facebook or Twitter. On the off chance that you make the prompt move to address any blunders, apologize freely and address remarks well, you convey to the world that your item or administration is worth their cash is that you are exceptionally proficient in serving your clients. It exhibits the trustworthiness of your business, and even though having to apologize may appear to be harmful, it is probably going to raise your notoriety whenever dealt with effectively. Clients feel esteemed and significant when their interests or objections are dealt with quickly and precisely, and web-based life permits you to demonstrate to try and still undiscovered clients that you are a business who can deal with such things with pride. Another way you can give your clients better encounters to advance your associations with them is by recognizing their commendations either by expressing gratitude toward them or suggesting other helpful items. Doing these two things, among others, gives your clients an incredible encounter and let them realize that you genuinely care about them. These straightforward advances outline for your clients how much you value them and demonstrate that you are eager to go the additional mile to guarantee that they can acquire some other items they may want

Chapter 1: The Basics Skill Building

This chapter will cover all the startup portion of SMM. Hopefully, the student will have fun while leering this chapter.

Investment Return:

It is the central subject that you simply finish this book. So be alarmed.

Or but be terrified not by learning the likelihood of ROI, yet the results of not evaluating the ROI.

If we are talking about Web, so the SMM just gauge the cash related return when a business, alliance, or individual devours money utilizing electronic systems administration media progressing.

This issue has expanded out of force in online life; there are confirmed nonattendance of surveying the regular effect.

The electronic experience came, pushed sort of a missile.

Likewise, quickly, every business expected to possess it in some structure.

Affiliations got hypnotized, helped along by the media introduction, and strengthen by associations that out of nowhere had another wellspring of pay. Surprisingly fast utilizing any methods, everybody was walking around the step. The difficulty is that no-one recognized the way to check ROI. Right now, got obtained work environments got selected; in any case, at that time, sometimes, the two individuals and affiliations got finished, as affiliations and affiliations began chatting with the solicitation: "okay, in any case, how is that this was impacting our compensation?" Publicity: "No, it's cold, man, online life is about obligation. "Business: "Great, what's the dedication?"

Exposure: "Goodness, it's cool. You leave utilizing online systems administration media, and it's beginning and end about the customer. It's sort of a customer-driven man; you meet people in several touch centres and lock-in. It's incredible."

Business: "all right, so how might it make us money?"

Advancement: "Better trust it, the open entryways are gigantic! You leave, and like make a Facebook page, and continue Twitter, and YouTube, and anywhere you'll. What's more, a short time later, you accompany people with a constructive brand understanding."

Business: "What's a real brand understanding? Does that raise the purchase point?"

Advancement: "Totally, man! Without a doubt, that's it. It lifts the acquisition plan."

Business: "Good, cool. So, what amount of salary did we produce once we paid you to draw in our group and lift to get the point?" Promotion: "Amazing, man that is feeling sort of highly contrasting. You must take a gander at the circumstance comprehensively. Individuals are investing a great deal of energy in online networking, so that is the place you should be, man."

Business: "I see. So, individuals make buys via web-based networking media?" Promotion: "Well, um . . . some of the time, I think. Be that as it may, pause, here's this truly fascinating infographic that shows all the informal communities individuals invest energy. Isn't it amazing?"

Business: "I assume. So, what does 'social impact' mean?" Promotion: "No doubt, I nearly overlooked! It's absolutely about impact. Better believe it, go out and distinguish the influencers. Ensure that you have an impact. It's everything about impact furthermore, the intensity of social referral."

Business: "You mean verbal promoting?"

Publicity: "Better believe it, absolutely, verbal promoting. Like alluding things, you like

to your friends. Boasting rights, sharing time, look at what I have, look at what I found."

Business: "All right, so how does that convert into really bringing in cash?"

Promotion: "Well, a few organizations are beginning to bring in cash . . ."

So, you sort of gets the image.

Social Media Marketing Skills

Paying little brain to how eagerly people are following the level of gainfulness of internet organizing, it's setting down profound roots. Moreover, it's similarly prominent that web-based life publicizing, as middle bent in modernized advancing, is a top capacity that gets people secured.

As demonstrated by LinkedIn, web-based systems administration displaying was the most sweltering skill that got people acquired in 2013

See

https://blog.linkedin.com/2013/12/18/the-25-mostsmokingcapacitiesthat-got-peopleenrolledin2013

Consistently the way they imply propelled publicizing seems to change, yet since 2013, progressed advancing (of which web-based life promoting is a middle part) has been at the top. The solicitation will waver after some time; be that as it may, we are examining the top aptitudes in any field to get people utilized.

2014: **https://blog.linkedin.com/2014/12/17/the-25-mostsultryskillsthat-got-individualsprocured in-2014**

2015: **https://blog.linkedin.com/2016/01/12/the-25-abilities that can-get-you-employed in-2016**

2016: **https://blog.linkedin.com/2016/10/20/top-abilities2016-weekof-learning-Linkedin**

The main thing which I have found during my line of work, that I try and strengthen in my books and my categories, is that the method that the central locus of robotized displaying area unit associated.

For example, I consider electronic life elevating to be in spades related to the positioning streamlining or SEO. In SEO, a central objective to induce a higher mission for motor rankings is to form and send substance to your web site that applies to your gathering, satisfactorily fitting to supply to others.

Similarly, wherever area unit people about to share it? Byways for electronic frameworks organization media. To boot, within the event that you simply expire a commentary or weblog section on your web site page, wherever may be superior to traditional spot to share it?

In this way, all I'm expressing is, many equivalents to some other inclination, web-based life exhibiting necessities to add to a business or affiliation unequivocally. Along these lines, ROI is a splendid idea to recollect a motivating point and discover anything about a thing.

B2B and B2C

There are likenesses in the manner you showcase items to organizations and purchasers, yet there are likewise contrasts. As a rule, a business to business, B2B, approach has a more extended deals cycle.

For instance, if you worked at a product organization and your activity was to fill out TPS reports, you may recommend utilizing outside support of assist load up with trip the stories.

You may go on the web, do some examination, and decide the expenses. You could go to a TPS supplier straightforwardly; however, you could likewise employ an office with the skill to exhort you.

So, you may have gatherings and present your proposition inside. Your manager may state, "Extraordinary thought, appears as though it costs a great deal; we should take a gander at this next quarter." In a quarter of a year, you return to the exploration, download a few whitepapers, and resume the procedure. At that point at long last, you contract a TPS organization.

It's not generally the situation, however regularly, there's increasingly content identified with somebody purchasing an item or administration for their business. For instance, if you end up offering independent web-based life showcasing administrations, or you work for an organization or on the other hand organization, you may entrust with assessing the new instruments available.

Right now, in a B2B circumstance, you see the material, assessing it, giving things a shot, and searching for surveys.

In a B2C circumstance, individuals additionally examine. However, it's occasionally not as dangerous. Furthermore, it probably won't take as long. For instance, on the off chance that you were looking for cell telephones, you may receive a gander at costs, or go to a store, read an audit, and make your buy-in half a month.

Interest/ PR

Duty could be a term you will have thought of, no matter whether or not it was indisputably within the speech before this minute. It existed before on-line life. Nonetheless, it's an unusual gift in electronic life. On an important level, with on-line life, you ought to "partner with" your gathering through kinds of progress, challenges, content, articles, and video. No matter it takes to induce people visiting with you and with you and talking with others.

It is a viewpoint of progressing. Its points of interest and rules. While not disconcerting such varied pointers or standards, I'll quit on a district and confirmation that devotion as a regular seemingly owes a lot to open relations than to no matter else.

The restriction of business, for the foremost half, has been to create a buzz a couple of factors. As an example, you will dream regarding holding a "presentation stunt," which attracted plenty of thought and joined to the presence of a set or factor.

On the opposite hand, you will have detected the verbalization, "advancing horrific dream," once one thing seems grating. Like this, a PR division's action is dependably to relate through no matter media channels they'll, and also much thought, the better.

The responsibility aspect of net-primarily based life may be smart of; in like manner, the goal is to induce thought. In any case, the request you, no matter everything, got to posture to yourself is, "What is that the impact on the business?"

In case you're attracting individuals with a snare, and they are locked in, does it convert into deals?

Possibly, perhaps not

With all the voice communication of ROI at the current time, it's smart for associate categorical that once unsure, and electronic life might contemplate, and presumably ought to observe, as open relations.

PR is often an unsuccessful price wherever you drive care-associated manage the name of an association.

Obscenity, in light-weight of the very fact that such a vital variety of individuals square measure via web-based networking media, it's pronounced that it's merely only hours, or maybe minutes before some bearish event transforms into a true "promoting awful dream" for any business.

It's in a like manner apparent that holding your ear to the bottom to understand provides early is an original plan. You'll call up that minute that little question regarding it "Watching" region later at the current time. Net-based mostly life cannot for posting; it's in like manner for calibration in (or poring over what others post regarding your association). Right once you are a business visionary, immense, or very little, you got to virtually guarantee that you just square measure out there searching for the web life world and square measure careful to something somebody says regarding your business.

WOM:

You may express that online life may be a phase fitting for "casual" displaying. The request is, are you able to genuinely "make" someone share a thing or wanted to, you just make it easier for them to try to like this?

For example, Apple Computer consumes money on display. Nevertheless, their centre intrigue is on making their things exceptional regardless. The enormity of their things takes on a significant a part of the contention of publicizing, and possibly considerably more. Since they (generally) produce first-rate things that customers love, people speak about them and educate others relevancy with them. It's self-actuated, verbal, promoting at its best.

All in all, what's the most working of a publicist, he will face with a thing that's just good, and the must-do "verbal" exhibiting? The short answer is that you simply can't accomplish something with anything.

To the extent of helping business, one amongst the assorted things that "social tuning in" can tell individuals' thoughts of your items. It's too certified that the most effective, best associations try their customers mindfully. One amongst the bounds an internet life sponsor can give has any reasonably affect a business makes and keeps their things astounding. Right after you try this, you get that unbelievable self-incited, verbal advancing.

Monitor the screen

Two or three people separate electronic frameworks organization showing and online life viewing. In any case, I'm putting them under a handy umbrella. Generally, there are various devices out there that facilitate yours with gazing at what individuals are communicating.

For instance, one in all the contraptions that are as frequently as conceivable sincere to online long-range relational correspondence advancing arrangements of necessities is Radian6, which is by and by a part of Salesforce.

Radian6 incorporates a full extent of brilliant approaches to managing to filter through electronic frameworks organization and envision the outcomes.

Radian6 will do things like allow you to know, accordingly, irrespective of whether individuals are feeling honoured or stunning about your image, ideas, and watchwords. There is a robotized side to web checking out viewing, and it's some worth, yet it in like way has its cutoff centres.

By considering everything, web checking out watching awards you to "check" electronic life and see what individuals are communicating, all the way down to the degree of individual posts.

Whole books are explaining social viewing, and we'll discuss it later within the paper, regardless, most significantly, you get what you obtain the right substance. Radian6 is dear. On the alternative fruition of the range, there are free instruments. In like manner, there are hundreds within the inside.

As an examination, have a go at visiting socialmention.com and making an affiliation name or applauded a human name to perceive what occurs.

Posting: Comments/Promotions:

Progress is that the spot most affiliations fail stunningly at content showing. They either suppose their development finishes once they've concentrated it (yet no one comes), or they place it on their social channels and suspend on for the qualifications (and changes) to return in. Heads up: Besides, within the event that you are unfathomably lucky, they will not (in any event while not some extra elbow grease from your social occasion). That is as a result of the net could be a jam-squeezed spot.

Moreover, recollecting that your substance could also be gorgeous, there is up 'til currently a colossal life of content out there clutching be found. You will, in like means, have to compile to see. However, people share content. It's periodically bound that one was persuading supply outcomes over the vary of going on offers.

Building Audience

You've quite recently done a considerable measure of group investigation, both in the substance method and ideation stages.

It is the spot all that laborious work starts to pay off.

The remote possibility that you've changed that assessment into content that decisively centres on the claim to fame swarm you recognized; you're starting at now well on your way to deal with building a relationship with that swarm. Going with techniques can help you with establishing that relationship.

Influence Market

Influencers are business venture execs. They are the people who've merely continuing large teams and have the speakers to contact those teams. They are those anyone you are trying to accomplish is presently standardization into it. Creating organizations with those influencers are in a different way to touch upon collect your assembly, and it's significantly unbelievable for publicists who're nevertheless trying to form their image affirmation and ill fame. Within the event that you simply have contended out your masterminding right, you may involve influencer advancing as a significant factor in your substance presentation method.

Comment Marketing

Remark advancing could be a little bit of relationship building, half content progress. There is an area unit many people (and bots) out there doing the diminish or reduce the prime type of this, primarily posting inessential remarks with joins on any journal section they will discover. That cannot right procedure; those remarks area unit habitually no-followed and might get you blocked from areas that are careful about post remarks. Since most on-line journals no follow their comments, in any case, it's nice to focus on the white-top approach to manage discernment propulsive that consolidates loads less relationship than you will guess. It's higher than swing interfaces along with your articles everywhere remark streams and discussions, scour the web for people United Nations agency area unit shaping intriguing things that area unit characteristic with all you are covering. By that time, you participate in an exceedingly spoken communication with them within the remarks. Currently, then, that merges presenting a relationship back on a connected article that you've got formed. Most occasions, it doesn't, it is several the time (if at no matter point) joins a notice of your things.

Guest Posting:

Your substance doesn't merely need to live on your site. With visitor posting, you make remarkable substance for another website with a related crowd yet a greater reach. Like remark showcasing, visitor posting has gotten unfavorable criticism as a result of the way many individuals were going about it is setting up whatever trash content, they could on any site with a semi-not too bad Domain Authority just to get joins.

Yet, visitor posting (progressed admirably) can be a super-amazing strategy to manufacture your position and extend your crowd. Visitor posting, like all types of relationship building, can be a great deal of work; however, in case you're posting in the correct spots, the potential for remunerations is high.

If you decide to go this course, you must find dependable destinations identified with your industry that will give you your byline. You can disclose to it's a decent site on the off chance that you'd be glad to send the connection to your chief or grandma (and not because it's a connection). At that point, compose intriguing and extraordinary substance that will urge individuals to search out increasingly content from you.

How to get started with guest posting

Guest posting looks a lot like comment marketing in the beginning:

1. Search for sites that have useful Page Authority and Domain Authority, as well as intense, relevant conversations (see above for more specific instructions).
2. Start commenting on posts and building relationships with those sites.
3. Pitch the editors of those sites with exciting blog post ideas that are tailoring to their sites. As you do this, avoid looking for the backlink. You're building authority, not links.
4. Promote anything you get published like crazy.
5. Repeat.

Outreach:

Another type of advancement that depends vigorously on relationship building is earning media, which regularly includes the effort to media and bloggers with a pitch for them to expound on you. In the two cases, you'll need to discover what the author or journalist is really intrigued by and cautiously tailor your pitches to ensure you're sending them things they'll find fascinating don't merely send them each and everything you've at any point made.

Often the individual on the opposite end will need something extraordinary on account of media; it's frequently early access to data or a restrictive, while bloggers may likewise be keen on complimentary gifts or exceptional arrangements for their peruses. Ensure you've perused any accommodation rules they may have before you approach them.

Social Media:

Because your substance is perfect for a specific crowd doesn't mean they'll see it over the span of their day. That is the place web-based life comes in.

On the off chance that your substance and social groups are firmly adjusted, at that point, you're now making the sort of material they need to share. Recollect that online life is more about relationship development than straight advancement, so anticipate that your social group should likewise share content other than yours. It is bravo since it can get new individuals taking a gander at your social channels.

Remember that you may have a great deal of data in your mind that could enable your social group to accomplish better reach. For instance, if you've composed an article that was the same as another article, send the social group the connection for the motivation and the contact data for the other essayist.

It additionally works on the off chance that you've cited somebody. You're giving your social group the unique situation and expansiveness of data they must prop the discussion up.

How to promote content with social media

Moz has a full social media primer, but you only need to know a few things to get started with social media promotion:

1. Choose the right channel. Some content is perfect for Facebook, some for Twitter, and some are great for both. You should know your audience well enough to have an idea of what they want to see where. If not, experiment.
2. Post at the right times. Facebook, Twitter, and LinkedIn all have some built-in analytics. And if you're using social media management tools like Sprout Social, Hoot suite, or Buffer, you should also have access to information about what days and what times of day your audience is most active. Use that to your advantage.
3. Use hashtags (prudently). Although hashtags are easy to overdo, they're also a way to get new eyes on the content you're posting on social. Research what hashtags are relevant for your industry and go (but not more than two at a time, please).

Paid Promotions:

Paid advancement covers a wide assortment of strategies from paid pursuit to show advertisements, paid social, and substance dissemination systems. Policies like these are frequently assembled under the umbrella of "pay-per-click" (PPC) promoting. Like web-based life showcasing, it is highly unlikely we can do the whole procedure equity right now, and we'll simply do a brisk diagram here to make you move the correct way. Make sure to characterize your crowd before you begin; that focusing on will assist you with getting more value for your money. Anthony Correggio, a PPC advertiser here in Seattle, composed an excellent introduction for that focusing on; we'd prescribe looking at it for more foundation.

Likewise, before you do any paid advancement, you should recognize your financial limit. Inside any channel, you can spend to such an extent or as meagre as you'd like. Knowing how much spending you need to play will help you recognize which channels you run on and which focusing on approaches you take.

Paid Social Media:

We realize that nobody has preferred information on us over the social stages we visit. We additionally invest gigantic measures of energy there.

So, from numerous points of view, it bodes well to partition out a portion of those advertisement dollars for content advancement on Facebook, Twitter, and anyplace else your crowd frequents on the Internet.

The more significant part of these stages let you redo who gets your promotions in very focused on ways, which can be a vast reward taken a gander at a buggy for a companion's infant shower? Get ready to see a promotion for it on Facebook. Looked at a charming end table? It may appear in an advanced tweet.

Now you as an advertiser can even transfer email records or use transformation pixels to make the resemblance to the other the same crowds that reflect the interests of the individuals on your current rundown, or who have seen your substance.

How to promote content with paid ads on Twitter

1. In Twitter, create a new campaign. Click on your account's avatar, then click "Twitter Ads." Twitter allows you to create campaigns based on your goals. If your content lives on your site, when setting up your new drive, choose "website clicks or conversions." It will allow you to get the most for your dollar, as the campaign will be targeted specifically to people who click through to your site.

2. Identify your targeting method. Twitter continues to release new ways to target a user on their network, each with positives and negatives. Test a few different options and see what works best for you.

3. When creating your ad, always include an image or video. Advertisements that display on a user's timeline always get more impressions and engagement when they have a visual asset.

4. Run more than one ad in each campaign, testing different creative elements and different calls to action. It will allow you to compare results and learn what went well and what can be improving during your next promotion.

Paid Research:

A paid inquiry is occasionally called "Internet searcher Marketing" (SEM) because it includes putting advertisements on web index results pages. It is an approach to get content before clients when they are hoping to settle on that buying choice. Two of the most well-known instruments/stages are Google Ad Words and Microsoft's Bing Ads.

At Moz we have found (and it is notable among the paid-search network) that SEM will result in overall capacity better as an immediate reaction publicizing instrument one that goes past basically connecting to a webpage or referencing a brand, and urges crowds to make a particular move, for example, pursuing a free preliminary or downloading an asset. It is not necessarily the case that it can't be utilizing to advance substance, yet to get the most traffic at the least value, we prescribe beginning with paid social pushes first, at that point attempting to fuse SEM channels.

How to promote content with paid research:

1. Work out your watchword list. These are the terms you need your promotions to appear for when a client looks for them.

2. Per your spending limit, recognize what match types you need to run. Precise match, where the client's question must match what you enter precisely for your promotion to show up, gives stricter focusing requiring little to no effort per click (CPC), yet will likewise send lower traffic volumes. Broad match brings more traffic volume. However, it has a higher CPC and looser focusing on that probably won't wind up throwing the opportune individuals your way. The choice you pick will rely upon how basic it is that your advertisement just shows for

individuals scanning for the specific term. In case you're Mitsubishi, for instance, and you're focusing on people studying for "Mitsubishi overshadow," you should restrain that to correct match, in case you wind up promoting your vehicle to individuals who were keen on space science.

3. Make a convincing promotion duplicate. You will serve promotions against natural and paid outcomes, and relying upon your offering, your advertisements may be in a lower position. Be as explicit in your promotions as could reasonably be expected: clients show expectations via scanning for exact inquiry terms. On the off chance that your advertisement is excessively broad, they won't lock-in. Also, on the off chance that you are offering gated (content that requires a stage from peruses typically giving their email addresses before they can see it), let that known in your promotion content. Make sure to underline that they will get a selective substance that others don't have.

4. At long last, guarantee that you're driving the traffic to an important, drawing in greeting page. On the off chance that we brought with the client and got them to tap in the promotion, you have won just a large portion of the fight. It's presently time to guarantee they draw in with your substance. Ensure you give the client precisely what you

have promised in your advertisement - at an opportune time, the point of arrival. Try not to make them look at a current landing page for what they need.

Display Ads:

Now and again alluded to as flag advertisements, show promoting permits you to put promotions (in a wide assortment of media from content to video) over the web utilizing a promotion server like Google Display Network (which shows Ad Words promotions) or Facebook's Atlas (which uses Facebook's focusing on information to put advertisements over the web). In case you're coming to content advertising from print news coverage, realize that even though we've taken the word, the idea of show advertisements is marginally extraordinary in computerized showcasing.

Show promotions are frequently utilizing in retargeting, where a client who has visited your webpage (as a rule demonstrated by a treat) at that point considers advertisements to be your website as they surf somewhere else on the web. For instance, on the off chance that you've taken a gander at a particular BBQ barbecue on Amazon, you may discover promotions for that flame broil on a blog you read, a news webpage, or even in your email stage, contingent upon what connections your advertisement server has with different locales.

There are a ton of approaches to alter retargeting, including term, recurrence, and particularity. You'll have to push the limits between potential clients, disregarding you and feeling stalked to death. That line differs, relying upon your industry. For instance, being retargeted by an undergarments store can feel much progressively self-evident (and meddling) than seeing a similar advertisement for a coffeemaker again and again.

Retargeting, as the paid pursuit, will, in general, get utilized for direct reaction endeavours, or, as a rule, getting individuals to join or buy your item. So, retargeting can be used in intriguing approaches to elevate your substance to profoundly qualified people.

Email Marketing:

Offering your new crowd individuals an approach to buy into your substance (or even only your updates) is an incredible method to ensure they hold returning, quickening the brand-building process.

One approach to do this is by gathering email addresses through a source of inspiration (CTA). You should send a month to month pamphlet to individuals who've communicated an enthusiasm for your substance, gathering together the best of what's occurred since the last release went out.

In case you usually delivering content with a similar fundamental organization (a blog, for instance), you can likewise set up an RSS channel that permits peruses to buy into your updates consequently. We'd suggest Feed Press as a necessary, economical arrangement. It offers fundamental examination so you can follow your endorsers and the achievement of what you're distributing and incorporates an adaptable pamphlet layout that you can use to make your messages fit your image.

The means to set up an RSS channel will shift a piece contingent upon your CMS. If you use something like WordPress or Drupal, it's imaginable as of now ready for action you simply need to plug the XML feed's URL into your feed director, change whatever settings you'd prefer to change, and later tear. In case you're utilizing a custom CMS, you may need to check with your designing group about guaranteeing the correct code set up before you make that stride. Feed Press and Feed Burner (Google's item) are both acceptable about making sense of your site, however, so give it a tear first.

Content Distribution Network

Regardless of whether you know it or not, you see the aftereffects of substance appropriation arranges always.

They're the perusing suggestions frequently found toward the finish of articles everywhere throughout the web in areas named "if you like this, at that point read… " or "you may likewise enjoy" These arrangements are generally paid and are moving through organizations like Taboola and Outbrain. It means your substance, as well, is qualified for this sort of dissemination.

One of the upsides of substance circulation systems is their enormous reach. You can likewise focus on your substance, determining what kinds of crowds you'd prefer to see it. A major hindrance is that some pretty nasty looking substance makers use them. You've seen these around: "Specialists don't need you to think about this one astonishing stunt to turn around maturing," or "Congrats! You fit the bill for decreased home loan instalments!" You can discover some comfort in the way that those people aren't likely focusing on similar gatherings you are (that is a case for incredible focusing inside itself), and at any rate, your work will stand apart as truly valuable

Chapter 2: Skill Therapy: Content Generation

This part examines content associated with web-based life, including contraptions you'll use to "do it without anybody's assistance." you'll consider it as a toolbox of capacities, or an expertise box. You'll take a journey through a neighbourhood of the items you ought to endeavour when working with online life.

Now and again, if you're working for an association, they will, starting at now, have systems likewise, content, similarly as any number of wellsprings of fabric, for introducing via web-based networking media. Regardless, there could be the occasional got to develop dynamically, outside of the quality systems. During a learning stage, it'll generally be valuable to understand the way to roll in the hay without anybody's assistance, so you'll get its vibe. You'll even get to start straight out, making "veritable" content as you're learning. The goal is to introduce a few of the thoughts and instruments that I accept merit having a go at, including for having material to figure with once you explore at online long-range interpersonal communication coordinates later within the book.

Curation vs Creation vs Collaboration

Curation:

Correctly once you serve content, you're going out and finding it, and a brief time was later sharing, looking over, and commenting thereon. You would possibly just aggregate and accumulate. Whether or not you are doing whatever it takes not to desire you've got an ingenious bone in your body, you'll leave and find material that may be fascinating and essential to your association. It is a straightforward technique to start. For instance, for a blog passage, you'll find an appointment of articles regarding a matter and form brief layouts/studies of them. You'll provide for the main items and subsequently offer an end. You'll find YouTube chronicles that relate to some extent and either accompany them or introduce them during a blog section. By then, you present your blog utilizing electronic systems administration media and make some traffic and care. You'll post substance, pictures, and chronicles genuinely to web-based life, yet the overall point is to urge some concern about your website page or blog.

Creation:

It is often the most straightforward time. It requires some investment, yet it frequently brings about the very best calibre.

Composing a piece of writing or blog entry or making a video, these are the simplest kinds of substance to share via web-based networking media, since they're one among a sort, and you'll tailor them to the gang. What type of content you create relies upon the organization or association yet start by asking yourself who the group is and considers what sorts of things they'd be keen on it? You'll ask individuals via web-based networking media or straightforwardly. It never damages to check your thoughts and find out what individuals have an interest in by going straightforwardly to them here and there. No matter whether you are not a media proficient, it tends to be useful to, at any rate, take a stab at the build-up some essential substance. You'll generally request that others survey your composition or a video you create. Giving it an attempt may assist you with being during a superior situation to "source" it. On the off chance that you simply finish up having the choice, it all right could also be smarter to consider what you are doing the simplest and contract somebody to conclude.

Collaboration:

I think this one is beneficial to remember, particularly for consultants, free entrepreneurs, and understudies. It all right could also be an approach to line aside cash and pool assets.

Discover individuals you'll work with, and it's going to be that you simply discover somebody who is an essayist, offer to co-keep in-tuned with some substance or do some examination, and obtain the advantage of their composing abilities or their notoriety. On the off chance that you simply got to make a video, you'll discover individuals who are keen on an identical result. You bring issues to light of a selected theme or identify individuals who got to have a go at something new merely, like you. Don't preclude anything, no matter whether you do not feel satisfied doing it without anyone's help, can't bear to contract anybody, and do not have the foggiest idea where to start. You'll have the choice to get individuals who hope to the team, no matter whether it's just for the training experience.

Creation of Google Account:

The Google account may be a Gmail account. You'll easily create a Gmail account for creating new and existing blogs by entering your name and age.

As a primary step, I like to recommend creating a free Google account by getting to http://mail.google.com and clicking Create Account.

Start your First Blog

There is an assortment of stages for blogging, yet blogger.com is one among the foremost effortless to utilize.

In case you're keen on creating web, based life promoting as a flair, my general recommendation is to form a blog and set the target of presenting thereon in any event once a month (or more frequently).

Pick some extent or device you're checking out about, or a technique you're keen on, do some examination, accumulate a couple of connections, and obtain susceptible to build up some progressing posts.

It'll help keep your abilities ebb and flow (counting examination), and it'll likewise be something you'll highlight at the purpose when you're attempting to urge customers or search for employment.

It is often useful to possess the choice to find out new apparatuses. Another explanation's valuable is because you'll finish up during a circumstance where a customer should make a blog, and you'll support them begin by being comfortable with and demonstrating them various apparatuses.

This equivalent guideline applies to some of the multiple instruments we're investigating this section. I suggest attempting them here and there. It's useful for building your range of abilities; however, it can likewise assist you with having the choice to point out a customer (or potential business) sometime soon. To begin, visit http://www.blogger.com and either check-in together with your Google record or snap the Create an Account connect at the bottom.

Check Pl

When you create the Gmail account, Just click on the blogger site as a "New Blog."

For training, don't be excessively worried about the title. You can transform it later effectively, and you can likewise make/erase no problem at all. Don't hesitate to attempt a "Web-based life Point of view" as a title.

The title used to show up outwardly at the highest point of the blog. The Address is the open-door Google offers you to make a custom location. Since it's a free apparatus, you may need to test a piece until you discover one that is accessible. Type in thoughts in the Address field, and see what occurs:

A custom portion of the blog address

It shows up for this model, and the location socialbuzznews.blogspot.com is accessible. The connection for this blog would be http://socialbuzznews.

www.blogspot.com

After you pick a title and address, you can select a layout for the look, what's more, feel of the blog, which you can likewise change later:

After you've chosen design (I prescribe beginning with Simple), click the Make Blog! Button. Utilizing these straightforward advances, you've made a blog and can start blogging!

Your strategy, you ought to decide to acknowledge it is to make an example post and, at that point, share the connection on Facebook or through email with somebody.

Variety of helpful articles is available

link: **https://support.google.com/blogger**

Find an honest Blog

I suggest that you simply take a stab at making a blog (and in any event, setting a suggestion to form a post once per month or more).

I likewise prescribe attempting to get a blog that you would be keen on perusing, as a case of "curating" content. Discover it on Google via trying to find something like "online networking websites." Discover a piece of writing that appears fascinating and make a note of the connection. At the purpose, once you make a Facebook page, you'll finish up wanting to post that interface on your page. Or on the other hand, you ought to make a connection to a different person's blog at the purpose once you are expounding on a topic.

Creation of Free Website

Regardless of whether you're build up your internet-based life nearness or chipping away at somebody else's, it all right could also be useful to think about making an "official" site for a venture, occasion, crusade, or customer.

A blog may be a site, and blogging stage, for instance, WordPress (www.wordpress.com), which has free and paid adaptations, have developed to where they will fill in as convenient web destinations, contingent upon how you mapped out them.

It tends to be more comfortable from the beginning to believe a blog as a spot you post "continuous" content, for instance, a library of articles, and your "primary site" is that the reference material which will not change as regularly, no matter whether it's for a business or association. In a corporation setting, realizing the way to make separate sites handily can likewise be a bit of social advertising, wherein case you create microsites. As an example, a corporation may have an exceptional advancement that shown via web-based networking media, what's more, Google advertisements. You'll have the choice to place it on the official principle site, yet, there may likewise be reasons where an exclusive microsite may be a superior thought. Microsites frequently utilize for uncommon advancements or offers. I feel Google Sites may be a suitable device for anybody making a primary site, and more instruments referenced toward the finish of this part. I prescribe you an effort to form a Google site and keep it as a feature of your stockpile. You'll even get to have a Google site be your original site, for instance, your independent business.

To begin, attend http://sites.google.com. Sign if you want to or click the Create Account button.

Like Blogger, Google Sites packs plenty of intensity. The opposite preferred position of destinations like Blogger and Google Sites is just in case you are not a designer, and you do not need to have specialized abilities to form sites utilizing these instruments. It's going to be an honest elective where you offer the help of concentrating on the substance for the web site or advertising and may prepare a place, without fundamentally having to use an internet engineer. There are limits, obviously, yet it can likewise be a beginning point. As an example, use Google Sites to accumulate substance in any case. At that time, mapped out and model, lastly, once you have a superior thought of where things are going, employ a planner/web engineer.

I think the equivalent applies to showcase microsites. Let's assume you build up a social media crusade and wish to possess a microsite. A massive piece of the fight simply built up the substance, gathering it in any case. You'll begin with a free device, take it as far as possible, and afterwards, choose if you want to have an increasingly flexible or but proficient looking structure. In this way, back to Google Sites.

Recollect how things change in internet-based life? They turn on Google also. Google tries and improves its items, and it's been testing with "Another" and "Exemplary" rendition of Google locales. you'll see a catch like this:

The chapter deals with the classic version.

(In case you're underestimating it how simple it is, have a go at going to Godaddy.com and taking a gander at how much exertion required to begin a facilitating account and get a site started, with a substance the executives framework like Drupal, a site manufacturer, or in any event, utilizing a manual instrument like Dreamweaver. I ensure after attempting that approach, and you'll acknowledge how much time you're sparing by merely being capable of clicking Create. Much obliged, Google.)

Much the same as with Blogger, Google Sites has pre-assembled formats you can pick from it. In Google Sites, it is somewhat more precarious to return and change things afterwards, so until you investigate how to alter your site, I suggest picking the Blank layout.

You can choose your desired template

You click in the Name Your Site field and type a name, which resembles a title and can be changed effectively later.

At that point, you'll need to analyze and attempt a unique "site area" name. You can likewise tap on Select a Theme or More Options. In any case, I propose keeping it straightforward at first. (In Google Sites, the "topics" are what you can return and effectively change later, and they give some necessary customization in look and feel.)

You likewise need to type in the CAPTCHA code, (for example, "bits" appeared in the figure) before you can tap the Create button.

As you're composing in site area names, Google may reveal to you that the one you need isn't accessible. Provided that this is true, you may need to continue attempting:

To learn more about Google Sites, go to either of these links, which point to the same place: **https://support.google.com/sites/?hl=en#topic= 1689606** or **http://tinyurl.com/googsite-help**

My first proposal is to make a site that features your portfolio and work understanding. You can likewise make a training site for a potential customer, such concerning a fanciful nearby business or a crusade or the like.

A system used to make websites

Several more popular options include free/paid options for building web sites:

- **http://wix.com**
- **http://weebly.com**

Create or Edit Video:

It's evident that whole books, or sets of books, could be expounded on every particular area of this part, yet I'm suggesting some straightforward beginning stages that are useful to investigate. With video, similarly, as with online journals and sites, you may wind up needing to employ an organization or expert to make a video as a significant aspect of a battle. Simultaneously, people can do lovely fascinating things all alone with something as necessary as an iPhone.

There is an assortment of approaches to make recordings, and on the off chance that you don't have a video camera or iPhone, I prescribe getting a more seasoned iPhone or only an iPod (indeed, they despite everything make them) to film video.

You can get a utilized iPhone reasonably efficiently, interface it to WIFI, and transfer recordings legitimately. As of this composing, even another iPod is $200, which can't be awful, with no month to month cell telephone bill. (It's likewise evident that a utilized iPhone utilized for making the video, what's more, some different uses, significantly over Wi-Fi.) If you've needed an iPad continuously, there are utilized alternatives there as well.

The explanation I suggest one of these choices for exploring different avenues regarding video is because it's straightforward, simple to utilize, make an excellent video, and you can transfer the footage legitimately to YouTube.

Getting acquainted with it, including making essential recordings, (for example, meeting somebody) and posting them on your blog or site, can be acceptable tests every single great approach to manufacture aptitudes and your portfolio. In additional proficient situations, regardless of whether you're mentioning a financial limit to employ a skilled videographer, you may, in any case, need to take a stab at prototyping your thoughts with less expensive methods of video.

Remember that the absolute most well-known recordings on YouTube created with extremely straightforward gear it's more about the thought than the hardware. I'm not Apple-one-sided, it's merely necessary, and that is useful for novices. Point and snap, and you can make essential recordings. At that point, you're a single tick away from being ready to transfer to YouTube:

Some portion of the explanation, proposing this sort of course of action is to keep the specialized issues to a base so you can centre around the substance.

The simpler it is, the better the time it is, the fewer issues there are, and the more certainty you will work from giving things a shot — only a beginning stage.

By examination, you can get a computerized camera with worked in video capacity, or any number of devoted cameras, load video altering programming on your PC, and afterwards move the video to your PC. I urge you to investigate that approach sooner or later.

Be that as it may, in the first place, I prescribe getting a modest iPhone or iPod or iPad, maybe one that isn't the most recent adaptation. Simply ensure it has worked in video. I'm recommending you attempt a few recordings without altering or just by utilizing YouTube's worked in the editorial manager. It means you shoot some small clasps on your straightforward cell phone and transfer them to YouTube. At that point, you alter them on YouTube. Honest, genuinely pure, and lets you centre around the substance.

Experience is that Apple sets aside a ton of effort to give a decent, straightforward, reasonably stable client experience, though, with the Android stage, it relies upon the maker.

The time you spend on making sense of things may detract from having some good times.

In any case, to set aside cash, or to dodge Apple explicitly, Android tablets are surely a decent choice. At the hour of this composition, you can get an Android tablet, with the ability to shoot video and transfer it to YouTube, for about $50.

Create or Edit the Video on YouTube:

My proposal can't make a lot about the video. Simply have a go at shooting "something," regardless of whether it's fundamental, and afterwards transfer it to YouTube. The YouTube Editor placed at https://www.youtube.com/proofreader. If you are new to Google Accounts or YouTube, you may need to set up a profile on YouTube:

Whatever YouTube recordings you've transferred to a specific record will show up, also, the YouTube Editor empowers you to do some fundamental altering on the web. I believe it's pleasant, regardless of whether there are limits, to have the option to give video by shooting a shot a versatile gadget, transferring straightforwardly, and afterwards altering in that spot on the web.

Similarly, as with different points, whole books could be composed of working with video, and you might need to take a gander at a few.

Be that as it may, I additionally urge you to analyze by making a straightforward short video and not stressing a lot over method yet. I figure it will give you certainty. Concerning internet-based life showcasing, I think the video is one of the most grounded, long hauls includes that will, in any case, be around as interpersonal organizations rise and fall. Getting acquainted with making recordings, regardless of whether they are unpleasant or fundamental or fundamentally educational, is something worth being thankful for

To become familiar with the YouTube Editor and how to utilize YouTube, visit https://support.google.com/youtube

Adjust Images

Another region I suggest investigating the motivations behind internet-based life advertising is advanced pictures. It can mean something as necessary as looking on

Google for pictures. When you discover a photo you like, you can right-tap on it also, spare it to your PC (Windows) or hold Ctrl down and click on the picture to duplicate it (Mac). Attempt some basic picture searches and practice with those pictures first. At that point, investigate sovereignty free picture assortments and administrations like clipart.com.

The fact of the matter is, in the long run, you'll presumably need to in any event have a go at playing with including pictures to a blog entry or site, and it's acceptable to realize how to function with photos or illustrations for presenting via web-based networking media. For instance, in any event, when you have a book-based post, a fascinating, related picture can prompt more consideration.

My suggestion is to have a go at making a blog entry about a specific theme, and either taking pictures or finding related images.

Even though when you transfer photos to sites or online journals, there are regularly working in "resizing" capacities, you despite everything, should attempt a device like www.picresize.com to edit a picture or resize it. (Take a stab at taking a gander at the assistance segment.) There are online apparatuses you can use, without fundamentally having to get familiar with an intricate picture altering programs like Photoshop (expensive) or Gimp (open source at **www.gimp.org**).

Take Pictures

For smiles, and to increase the value of your blog entries, I suggest learning the most effective method to take screen captures, particularly understudies and assistants, or anybody for that matter. Consider it a way of taking pictures on the web. For instance, most of the movies right now composing are screen captures, where I'm making an image of something and afterwards talking about it. Counting a copy of a bit of programming or a site is a simple method to add a visual to squares of content. Greens hot is without one instrument you can attempt at **www.getgreenshot.org**

You're crucial you decide to acknowledge it is to pick an element in something like Blogger or Google Sites, or even Facebook, investigate it, take a screen capture, or on the other hand, two of it and put them in a blog entry.

Conclusion:

This part has unquestionably been a tornado. There is a lot of remaining details. In any case, my methodology is to assist you in beginning such that is basic and fun. On the off chance that you've been looking through it, I prescribe experiencing the part more cautiously, perhaps attempting one device daily, or every week, and getting something going, for instance. As you try internet-based life-promoting, you'll need to have material to rehearse with, so it's better on the off chance that you can have a go at making your very own portion test substance to put something aside for future models.

Chapter 3: Facebook Pages

The objective of this part is to present the thought of Facebook pages and to inform the tactic of creating a Facebook page effectively. On the off chance that you simply haven't made a Facebook page previously, I suggest giving it an attempt, no matter whether you do not have an "official" venture yet. Similarly, like many free devices nowadays, you'll return, what's more, erase it.

Introduction to Facebook Page

A Facebook page may be a focal "centre point" for a business or non-benefit association to line up an internet-based life nearness on Facebook. It's necessarily like having an internet site page or site of your own, however "inside" Facebook, and following its design. As a Facebook page proprietor, you'll make posts of various sorts, counting content, pictures, video, then forth., and if clients click the likes of catch on the page, at that time, in theory, they're going to get posts in their newsfeed once they check in to Facebook. Most web-based life advertisers consider a nearness on Facebook a must-have; however, it merits knowing the cutoff points and expenses, as we'll talk.

Standard Facebook pages incorporate ones about writers, motion pictures, and amusement. As an example, if you continue Facebook and sort "lattice" within the hunt box, you'll choose "The Matrix" Facebook page. As of now, it's around 7 million individuals who've preferred it.

Facebook pages additionally have "web addresses," which may be utilized in unique materials to publicize or hook up with the page. As an example, the immediate connection to "The Framework" Facebook page is https://www.facebook.com/TheMatrixMovie. At the purpose, once you get to a Facebook page, contingent upon how things are

Structured, you'll, by and enormous, observe a clear picture at best, a container with the Profile symbol, and a territory for posts beneath it.

Notice the "Include a Cover" picture. That's one among the alternatives for tweaking your Facebook page, which pushes, a prod may be a chance to figure with exceptional views, as depicted within the last part. At the purpose, once you begin making profile symbols or spread pictures, it's entirely expected to start with a map and afterwards resize it/crop it to selected size. Here may be a case of a Facebook page that I loved. Since I preferred it, a post appeared in my newsfeed.

Notwithstanding diversion and business, over the first recent few years, Facebook pages have likewise progressively been worked around causes and have had an immediate effect on world occasions, both through official pages of developments, also as free pages. As an example, during the Arab Spring, I made a Facebook page with a couple of music and verse to empower individuals who were fighting to realize big government within the nations in the Middle East. Look at

www.facebook.com/freedomsongs

You may be intrigued to survey/examine the idea of how the insurgency in the Middle East started. It wasn't "caused" by social media, yet incidentally, a Facebook page was a focal technique of correspondence.

http://www.nytimes.com/2012/02/19/books/surv ey/how-an-egyptian-upsetstartedon- facebook.html

It was the page that necessarily begun it:

https://www.facebook.com/elshaheeed.co.uk

You may likewise be keen on taking a gander at a video I made, which visits the "Opportunity Songs" Facebook page I made on the side of the insurgency, with a conversation of how Facebook publicizing was utilized.

It additionally incorporates some of the "in the background" data on the Facebook page, including measurements that were accumulating about individuals who visited and enjoyed the page from different nations.

The title is "How to Start a Revolution (or Help One)," and an immediate connection is **http://tinyurl.com/fb-arabspring**

Facebook Pages: Do's and Don'ts

As I would like to think, one of the most significant focuses to remember about Facebook pages, regardless of whether you are making one for a business or non-benefit association, are the confinements. Facebook pages frequently viewed as a focal bit of online life procedure, and the general mentality is that they are an unquestionable requirement have. Notwithstanding, some functional changes at Facebook have changed the viability of pages as a limited time device, which merits taking a gander.

Facebook Business Model

One thing that helped me during a book I examine Google (Winning AdWords by Danny Sullivan) was a test that Sullivan made about the comprehension of Google's plan of action. I figure a comparable standard can support web-based life advertisers take a gander at Facebook with a great eye.

For Google's situation, the conversation was about methods for getting a page recorded on Google's web index for nothing, which is otherwise called SEO, or Search Motor Optimization. Google permits just about any site to registered for free of charge, yet it additionally offers the open door for paid ad. (The paid promotion understood as program Marketing or SEM).

As far as plans of action, Google doesn't usher in cash from offering a free position on its internet searcher. At the purpose when individuals submit joins, and

at the end, when Google slithers the web to seek out destinations, consequently, it includes esteem to Google. Notwithstanding how Google makes most of its cash is thru promotions. Many billions of dollars in promotion income.

So the test is that no matter whether you set exertion into the "free" strategies, it is sensible that Google's plan of action about paid to publicize, which investing assets and energy into the paid strategies are progressively supportable what's the more, reliable end of the day.

As per Google policies, it doesn't "guarantee" anything because it knows of the very fact that the entire industry developed around SEO.

Albeit the free Google position, SEO, are some things to be thankful for to try to, you cannot depend upon it.

On occasion, Google will change how sites show up, which may have a quite enormous effect on organizations that have made suspicions about their "free" Website design enhancement battles. to place it plainly, understanding where a business brings in cash can assist you with arranging the end of the day and contemplate advertising in its "channel." As far as online networking, verifiably what happened is that Facebook developed, and afterwards began considering the way to usher in cash, which eventually directly affected Facebook pages.

The certain suspicion wants to be that once you got individuals to love your Facebook page, the posts you made would show up in their newsfeeds.

Quite a sort of membership. Online life touted as a technique where you'll just about get free publicizing self-advancing via "web-based networking media" and, at that time, assemble a nearness by putting content out there.

In any case, at that time, Facebook began charging for "boosting" posts. I feel the essential rule applies to Facebook also.

Simply remember the question of how Facebook brings in cash? The acceptable response is through publicizing. So, all things considered, while you'll get something to without stopping, at last, it probably won't be manageable, and it's imperative to possess practical desires. With web-based life, it's particularly essential to think basically, and incredulously, on account of all the publicity around it. So, as a web-based life advertiser, you'll have customers who know "they need to have an internet-based life nearness," and you'll have the choice to assist them hooked into this "must-have" demeanour. After some time, I think it's imperative to pose an inquiry about the degree of profitability and comprehend what the effect is. You would like to deal with suppositions that individuals have and assist them with understanding the real worth. At last, take a gander at the numbers.

So, I may make the suspicion that on the off chance that I post something, in principle, the individuals who like the page would get the post in their newsfeeds. (Despite whatever they do, there's no assurance of everybody peruses every one of their jobs, which is another confinement of Facebook that is critical to remember.)

So, I make posts and trust in the best.

The significant inquiry to pose is what number of individuals observed the post? At the point when you post to your page on Facebook, you can perceive what number of individuals it was "served."

The red bolt calls attention to the moderately new Facebook "highlight," which permits you to support the post. You'll rapidly perceive how to contact more individuals, and you need to pay Facebook.

Indeed, right now," "Facebook includes an approach to reach additional individuals past your crowd. Be that because it may, it's additionally charging you to contact individuals who loved your page. So, on the off chance that you simply thought arriving at your fans was free, reconsider.

Posts Boost:

From my point of view, I feel it finishes up being like Google promotions. There's rivalry, and to a limited degree, it resembles Facebook is treating individuals' newsfeeds like Google list items. You'll pay Facebook to point out signs of improvement change of being taken note.

When you finish writing everything, it's useful to recollect how things are getting to work. There is no rule out any case; it merits testing.

A couple of organizations have had achievement learning adherents and utilizing Facebook pages to assist found out and continue their essence via web-based networking media. From a validity point of view, many contend that some portion of maintaining "social believability" has a web-based life page.

Be that because it may, there are additional examples where the exertion and cash put into a Facebook page prompts faulty outcomes. as an example, here's a piece of writing where somebody looked with a big eye, did some testing, and discovered that Facebook pages, for them, weren't such a sensible thought:

http://www.forbes.com/destinations/elandekel/2013/01/22/facebook-pages-are-aterriblespeculationforsmall-organizations/

At last, I feel that Facebook pages are certainly worth checking out. They're genuine centres for web-based life. I prescribe considering Facebook an analyze it. It provides it with an attempt and perceives how it functions.

At that time, take a gander at the numbers. no matter whether you never posted them via web-based networking media, they might be significant. (To some extent, since they assist a site, get acknowledgement on Google.

As such, albeit SEO has its restrictions, merely putting content on your site draws individuals there and causes you with Google indexed lists.) If you, as of now, have the substance, why not share it via web-based networking media? Just recollect to "drill down" and take a gander at what number of people are observing it to line reasonable desires. Some portion of your online networking system may include attempting various methods for expanding commitment, for instance, making a video that has got to a better degree an opportunity of being shared as a result of its allure the story, the diversion, the importance of knowledge. An identical thought applies to articles. The most concern is internet-based life merits attempting.

Creating a Facebook Page:

Creating a Facebook page is relatively straightforward. Just go to **https://www.facebook.com/pages/create**

to get started

Clicking the company type

Choose Category

Write the name of the business

Next, you will drive through a progression of screens where you can enter essential

data.

As a learning exercise, I suggest making an agenda that you can allude to collect this substance afterwards. Be that as it may, for the present, I recommend tapping the Skip button on each page:

The next screen allows you to choose the photo

It is presumably worth doing. It just makes your page more straightforward to discover and oversee at the point when you sign in to Facebook. Top picks allude to your "Top choices" territory on the landing page when you sign into Facebook, until/except if Facebook changes its arrangement:

At that point, you get a prologue to Facebook promoting, finishing with welcoming you to make a promotion. How does Facebook bring in cash? Through promotions.

As you'll find in Chapter 4, there's an assortment of approaches to make a promotion. I prescribe I was avoiding this page until further notice.

Then you have a draft Facebook page

More things Change

Another point I think is beneficial to recollect is that Facebook and other internet-based life channels regularly change their highlights, frequently out of a craving to enhance or be progressively secure.

Therefore, the way that Facebook pages work may change (for instance, there weren't initial spread pictures), the interface utilized to figure with them may change, or extra highlights will include.

My general recommendation is to research Facebook and survey assistance. Facebook frequently sends messages with refreshes also. Find out the way to learn and do not be hesitant to investigate as new highlights end up.

Conclusion

All the simplest in investigating Facebook pages! My general proposal is to consider the substance and not the channel, for instance, Facebook. Once you are creating content, explore different avenues regarding presenting it on various online life channels. Use Google to scan for articles that mention internet-based life technique, counting what to post, how regularly to post, and so on. A sheltered principle is to believe what your crowd would be keen on perusing.

Make sure to consistently perceive what number of people you're coming to together with your posts!

Chapter 4: Ads on Facebook

This section is a prologue to Facebook advertisements, which ordinarily utilized for web-based life advertising. There is some conversation in the sort of ads and the customary benefit of using them. It is just as certain things that have changed on Facebook as new kinds of promotions have presented. You additionally have a chance to make a Facebook promotion. You will promote a blog or webpage you made in the wake of perusing Chapter 2 or use Facebook promotions to publicize a Facebook page that you made in Chapter 3. My suggestion is to make or find a site that you need to broadcast a piece, make a promotion, and have a go at running it for a week or somewhere in the vicinity. We are close to the finish of this part; we check the glance of "checking" Facebook promotions and how to assess their presentation.

What is Facebook Add? And Why we use it?

The most common type of Facebook ad is the kind that appears on the right side of the page when you log in to Facebook. Here are some examples.

Another type of advertisement shows up straightforwardly in your newsfeed, close by posts from your companions and from Facebook pages that you have preferred. At the top, it says Suggested Post:

You shouldn't be a business offering an item or administration to utilize Facebook advertisements; anybody can use them. For instance, I made this little advertisement to check whether I could draw a few people into perusing a sci-fi short story:

It prompts a site called Wattpad. I wasn't selling anything fundamentally, and I was simply advancing some fiction that I had composed:

When you are using Facebook Ads

The main concern on Facebook advertisements is that within an inexpensive timeframe, individuals are so far investing an excellent deal of energy on Facebook. There's proof to recommend that younger individuals are investing more energy in informing applications like Snapchat, WhatsApp, et al. , and investing less energy in Facebook (since their guardians are on it?), however toward the day's end, individuals are so far spending an excellent deal of your time on Facebook.

So, one guideline about Facebook promotions, and any kind of internet-based life showcasing, is that it "accepts the way things are." That is, anywhere, individuals are investing in energy.

Regarding when to utilize Facebook promotions, there's not such a lot a group in stone time; in any case, the foremost widely known utilizations incorporate while advancing Facebook pages, where the promotion is on Facebook, it is shown to Facebook clients. Therefore the objective is to urge individuals to go to the Facebook page and snap the likes of catch.

As talked about in preceding sections, one necessary inquiry to pose is whether you're getting an arrival on the venture from something sort of a Facebook page. If you or your customer has the target of "expanding likes," at that time, a Facebook advertisement may be a decent method to urge a web-based life nearness built up.

What I've seen professionally may be a trend toward using Facebook ads for "customary" show promoting, which suggests utilizing a billboard on Facebook to spotlight a free site, with an image and content.

It's a case of covering with "customary" Internet promoting and web-based life advertising.

In customary Internet promoting, a presentation advertisement may show abreast of a news site, as an example, and comprise of an image or activity and content, which highlights an area.

Informal communities tagged along, and online networking showcasing was conceived. The overall objective and extent of internet-based life advertising are to create up and continue a nearness via web-based networking media. Be that because it may, a Facebook advertisement is often utilized for "customary" purposes, too; it's going to be all right to publicize a site.

It is a topic worth talking about or in any event, discussing, and a few contend that any nearness on the web is inherently social, which online networking advertising assists organizations with the understanding that the new time of customer association is increasingly on the brink of home. It could contend that a "customary" site may be a piece of a substantial internet-based life nearness.

Purchase Intent

I think another critical principle when considering Facebook ads is that the question of procurement aim. Beat all, setting a billboard on an internet search tool isn't quite an equivalent as setting one on a "general" site.

Individuals are sure to continue Google or other web search tools once they are looking into an item mostly once they expect to shop. While it'd change after a while, it's, for the foremost part, acknowledged that individuals are, for the first part happening Facebook to perceive what their companions are up to or to post material, not really to form buys. Some presents sum on social referrals, for instance, "hello, look what I have" or "hello, I prescribe this." In any case, it's so far, the case that the buy purpose is presumably altogether less than with web indexes.

This goal means measurements, albeit there's, to a lesser degree, an opportunity of a buy when on Facebook, promoters, despite everything, place advertisements there. The measures could be lower on getting steals. However, it can, at present, occur only something to recollect.

Metrics of Measuring Facebook Ads

While checking out about Facebook advertisements, there are a couple of ideas that are worth considering. Facebook and other advertisement stages show an excellent deal of knowledge at the purpose when you're running a billboard crusade.

You do not get to know all the aspects of interest in utilizing them. I suggest investigating and considering this to be an examination. The more you employ Facebook advertisements in business settings, the more you will be keen on some of the higher focuses after a while.

Check Plagiarism Check Grammar

The main reason for the promotion is to get individuals to tap on it and to visit a specific page or site. Another idea to consider is the active clicking factor. It's otherwise called CTR. For instance, in the accompanying figure, you can find in the Reach classification that in the hypothesis, the promotion shows to 61,432 individuals. There were 81 ticks. So, the active visitor clicking percentage was .081%.

The active clicking factor gives you an approach to taking a gander at execution. You may begin with a specific active visitor clicking percentage, or you may make a stab at having various forms of a promotion, with multiple pictures and content, and see which gives you a better active clicking factor.

Target Ad:

Another focal idea in advertisements is focusing on arranged it.

At the point when you make an advertisement on Facebook, you can pick explicit crowds, and the more focused on your ad is, the better it will perform as a rule. The more your promotion is centred around speaking to a specific crowd, the better it will do. Some portion of the focusing on process is simply the advertisement. In a fundamental model prior, I incorporated a few expressions about the story I composed, which may be of intrigue to individuals who like sci-fi:

In the Targeting segment of Facebook, I picked individuals who communicated a conspiracy in sci-fi in their Facebook profiles. I additionally picked a specific geographic region and language:

Creating Campaign:

https://www.facebook.com/business/a/campaign-structure

Click on Create an Ad.

From time to time, Facebook will change its interface. At the time of this writing, the wizard allows you to choose from various kinds of ads. I suggest trying the Page Likes or Clicks to Website options:

With the Clicks to Website advertisement, you give the connection to a site you need to send individuals to, (for example, the blog you made in Chapter 2).

Simply enter the link and press enter

(Note: When you enter the connection, it might flip you to another page even previously you click Continue.)

On the following page, you'll have the chance to do some focusing, by picking what crowd you need the advertisement to show to:

As you settle on decisions on the left side, the Audience Definition on the right side will refresh progressively:

It is a fascinating region to explore different avenues of favours. To begin, have a go at entering language alternatives.

At that point, take a stab at entering Interests. It is the place you can truly concentrate on a specific crowd. In case you're monitoring the numbers, you'll see that at the hour of this composing, you begin with around 184,000,000 individuals you can send a promotion to if you don't target them by any means.

These are the individuals who communicate in English in the US who are likewise on Facebook. When you begin entering interests, the numbers go down.

Individuals who take demonstrated a specific intrigue before enjoyed a page that falls inside a particular classification and so on. There's a little potential pool, yet this is something to be thankfully aimed. The promotion is more focused on, so individuals who see it are bound to tap on it, at any rate in principle.

Next, you get into the Account and Campaign area. Planning for Facebook promotions is a craftsmanship and a science. There are no all-inclusive rules.

However, an essential standard is that the more rivalry there is for a specific crowd, the more the promotions will cost.

One technique for paying for advertisements depends on the amount, that is, the number of developments that are shown. The other method is the place you pay just for clicks that happen. It is a territory that occasionally experiences changes, yet the fundamental thought is you make sense of a calendar the amount you're willing to pay and afterwards set it moving.

Conclusion

Congrats on enduring the section. The most uncomplicated guidance I can give on checking out about Facebook promotions is to research them, give them an attempt, and spend a while within the assistance areas on Facebook. I likewise recommend keeping things basic. It all right could also be an excellent deal of amusing to ascertain the snaps begin getting through the first time you attempt, which may generally prompt getting conversant in the highlights and choices that help cause your advertisements to perform better.

In case you're an assistant or understudy, plan to discover a site and set the target of seeing what number of snaps you'll get. At that time, try again to see whether you'll consider additional convincing pictures or content, or increasingly engaged that specialize trendy. See what your unique active visitor clicking percentage was and check whether you'll improve it. You would possibly get to begin posing the inquiry, "what's my ROI?". just in case you're intrigued in selling something, you will need to start out investigating a topic called transformation, which is following a billboard right down to the purpose of really selling something.

Chapter 5: YouTube

Not within the smallest degree, as other easygoing correspondence stages, YouTube simply has video content. If you are making a YouTube channel to trade one video easily and haven't any point of maintaining the stage, you ought to reevaluate.

You'll have to place aside plenty of your time to set up, film, alter, highlight, and separate your substance on a trustworthy explanation. You'll besides got to depict your image's objectives and plan for a way video can explicitly assist you with accomplishing these. On the off chance that you simply can present an appropriate extent of your time and centrality into the stage, you will have the selection to form partner with, shareable substance for your making swarm.

How to create YouTube Channel

Before you start recording video content, you will have to line up your YouTube channel. It will get somewhat tangled. As you were more likely than not know, YouTube ensure by Google. Right now, you search for after a Gmail account, and you accordingly get to a YouTube account, a Google+ record, and liberally more.

Subordinate upon your business, you presumably won't have any desire to hitch your email to your business' YouTube channel, particularly on the off chance that you simply need to give access to the record to accomplices or an office associate. We propose that you simply make a typical email account which will be utilized by various individuals.

- To begin, visit Google and snap "Sign in" within the upper right-hand corner.
- Snap-on "Make a record" at the bottom of the page.
- You'll see an elective originate from forming a record for yourself or from affecting your business. Since your YouTube record is going to be for your business, pick "To affect my business."
- To formally make your Google account, enter your name and required email and puzzle express before clicking "Next." At that time, join a recuperation email and your birthday, original bearing, and phone number. Note: Google requires all clients to be in any event 13 years aged.
- Finally, consent to Google's Privacy Policy and Terms of Service and check your record with a code sent using a substance or call. Well done! You're legitimately the fulfilled proprietor of a Google account.

Create YouTube Brand Account

Since you've got a Google account which you are mostly organizing to spread some excellent video content. In any case, we're not done at now. You, at present, got to found out a YouTube Brand Account. A Brand Account licenses clients to regulate modifying endorsements and make an inflexibly generally comprehensive on the online closeness.

- To begin, visit YouTube. within the upper right-hand corner, note that you're more likely than not as lately set apart into your new Google account. (If no vulnerability about it, "Sign in" and enter your new Google account username and secret word.)

- At the purpose when you've separate in, tap your record module and snap "My channel" within the menu.

- By and by, you need to induce to form a Brand Account. Enter your Brand Account name and press "Make." Note: you'll generally restore or change your channel name from your record settings, don't likewise, worry if you are not 100% secure together with your picked mark.

Guidelines

Your YouTube channel is an improvement of your image, and it needs to treat therein limit. As you create and alter your channel, hold close these YouTube brand administers so you'll appropriately found out your channel's character and begin to tug in supporters.

Your channel name said to each video your suitable assurance its benefit and obvious together with your other web checking out objectives and everyone things considered checking.

Google suggests moving an 800 x 800 px square or round picture. Your channel picture seems like a Facebook profile picture. This picture is going to be utilizing over the entire of your Google properties, for instance, Gmail and Google Plus. Think about using an affiliation logo or, just in case you're an open figure, an expert headshot.

Transfer a 2560 x 1440 px picture, which will scale overflow the central part of a neighborhood, tablet, advantageous, and TV. No one can inform you where your gathering will see your records.

Your depiction should give more data on your affiliation and clarify what kind of video content you propose on sharing.

Web search gadgets take a gander at your portrayal while finishing the way to rank your profile, so join relevant catchphrases in your format. We'll speak intelligently about the way to improve express video depictions underneath.

Your trailer needs to be rapid and straightforward (around 30 to 60 seconds). Consider displaying guests what your channel is about and what they will decide to find in your records. Make some extent to urge them to shop for something. Your trailer won't be obstructed by sees, which can keep the client targeting why they ought to observe more records from your image.

Your channel could be prepared for a custom URL just in case you've got quite 100 endorsers, a channel picture, channel craftsmanship, and is over 30 days old. Get to understand custom YouTube URLs here.

The station joins Link to entirely or any other web arranging records and material regions from the "About" a part of your position. Make it direct for supporters to collaborating with you elsewhere

Video Optimization

Since your YouTube channel is entirely operational, we need to mention solicitation improvement.

Recall how we referenced that YouTube is that the second most prominent web searcher? While making a pulling in the content may be a level out a need, it's clear, by all record, not by any means the sole factor for progress. There are two or three belongings you can do to enhance your narratives to rank staggeringly on both YouTube and Google recorded records.

The first development to becoming a YouTube showing genius is making and refreshing your video's metadata. Metadata gives watchers data about your video, which mixes your video title, depiction, marks, class, thumbnail, captions, and shut inscriptions.

You are giving the right data in your video's metadata guarantees that are fittingly mentioned by YouTube and show up when individuals are watching for accounts like yours. Be conservative and obtain when adjusting your metadata; your substance might be expelled if you plan to push it with irrelevant watchwords. Check out the video underneath to urge settled with overhauling your video for search.

Title:

Much like with on-page SEO, it's essential to refresh your video's title and portrayal.

Titles are what individuals initially read while rummaging through a review of records, so ensure yours is palpable and convincing it should intrigue searchers about your substance or make it evident that your video will assist them with managing a problem. Improve comprehension of what watchers are trying to find. Review the foremost central data and watchwords for the beginning of your title. Considering, keep titles to around 60 characters to shield content from being stopped in results pages.

Description:

YouTube will just show the hidden a couple of lines (around 100 characters) of your video's outline. To research past that, watchers should click "Show more" to ascertain the remainder. Thus, dependably merge imperative affiliations or CTAs on the brink of the beginning of your delineation and make the duplicate, so it drives perspectives and duty.

Underneath this, join the video transcript. Video transcripts can incredibly improve your SEO because your video is often flooding with catchphrases. Fuse a default channel depiction that mixes relationship with your social channels, video credits, and video-unequivocal time stamps. You'll additionally meld #hashtags in your video titles, and depictions simply attempt to utilize them sparingly.

Tags:

Next, include your standard watchwords in your marks. Marks accomplice your video with equivalent chronicles, which augments its range. While naming chronicles, name your most noteworthy slogans first and endeavour to fuse a mean mixture of progressively regular catchphrases and long-tail catchphrases.

Category:

After you progress a video, YouTube will allow you to select a video arrangement under "Front line settings." Video classes pack your video with the related substance on the stage. YouTube permits you to sort your footage into one among the going with arrangements:

Film and Animation, Autos and Vehicles, Music, Pets and Animals, Sports, Travel and Events, Gaming, People and Blogs, Comedy, Entertainment, News and Politics, How-to and elegance, Educations, Science and Technology, and Nonprofits and Activism.

Thumbnail:

Video thumbnails are the crucial pictures watchers see while glancing through a summary of video results, and yours can massively affect the proportion of snaps and points of view your video gets. YouTube will auto-produce several thumbnail decisions for your video. In any case, we eagerly propose moving a custom thumbnail.

YouTube reports that "90% of the simplest performing chronicles on YouTube have custom thumbnails". When recording, consider first-class shots that accurately address your video. YouTube recommends employing a 1280 x 720 px picture to make sure that your thumbnail looks fantastic on all screen sizes. Note: you ought to check your YouTube record to manoeuvre a custom thumbnail picture. You'll do that by visiting youtube.com/affirm and entering the check code YouTube sends you.

SRT Files:

Not solely do subtitles and shut engravings help watchers. Anyhow, they, in like manner, help streamline your video for search by permitting you another opportunity to spotlight noteworthy catchphrases. You'll incorporate inscriptions or shut legends by moving a maintained substance transcript or facilitated subtitles record. You'll, in like manner, provides a full transcript of the video and have YouTube time the inscriptions normally, type the subtitles or understanding as you watch the video, or agreement a specialist to unravel or decipher your video.

To incorporate inscriptions or shut captions, head to your channel and Snap-on "YouTube Studio," YouTube's exchange for Video Manager.

Once inside your YouTube Studio, click "Accounts" on the left menu. Find the video to which you've got to include inscriptions or closed subtitling and snap on the title to open the video settings.

Open the "Moved" tab and pick the video language. At the purpose, once you choose a word, the selection to "Move Subtitles/CC" should open. Tap that other option and prefer to move your inscriptions or shut recording with or without timing.

As against clarifications, YouTube urges customers to meld cards and end screens in their chronicles to review watchers, association with external areas, or direct people to varied records.

Cards and End Screen:

Luckily, cards and end screens are as easy to incorporate as clarifications. Tickets are pretty much nothing, rectangular notification that appears in the upper right-hand corner of both work zones and versatile presentations. You can consolidate up to five cards for every video, yet on the off chance that you incorporate different cards, make a point space them out similarly to give watchers time to make the perfect move.

Cards aren't yet available on YouTube Studio. To incorporate cards, click "Producer Studio Classic" in the left menu to follow these methods.

Playlist:

Is it exact to state that you are making chronicles around several particular subjects? Playlists might be the perfect device for you! Playlists grant you to serve a combination of records from both your channel and various channels.

Notwithstanding the way that playlists help to organize your channel and urge watchers to continue viewing equivalent substance, yet they furthermore show up freely in filed records. Making playlists gives you an undeniably discoverable component.

To cause another playlist, to go to a video you'd want to incorporate and click "+Add to" under the video. Next, select "Make another playlist." Type for the playlist you have to feature and snap "Make."

Writing Video Script

Goal setting

Like for any great battle or distributed substance, it is essential to create up what you would like to realize together with your video before you get into the stray pieces of breathing life into it.

Would you wish to create mindfulness for your image? Drive inbound site traffic? Add endorsers of your channel? Increment social offers? Or, on the opposite hand, accomplish something different altogether?

Setting up a solitary objective toward the start of the creation procedure is critical and can permit you to centre the video's content and technique on achieving it.

It's consummately okay to have different objectives for your YouTube channel, like expanding brand mindfulness and including supporters, yet the most straightforward practice is to consider one goal for each video.

Creation of Story Board

When you've built up the target for your video, placed on your inventiveness cap, and start handling your storyboard. A storyboard resembles an idea for your video and fills in as a framework for the shoot.

You've presumably even observed one preceding. Storyboards appear as if funny cartoons and incorporate harsh representations of varied scenes combined with short expressive data about the scene, camera position and movement, and exchange. they modify within the degree of detail included, however, your storyboard should, in any event, include:

- A casing for every significant scene or area change
- Essential unmistakable data about the scene (time of day, climate, mind-set of the characters, then forth.)
- Lines for each scene
- Camera bearing for movement and shot subtleties (for example tight, medium, or wide shots)

Additional Elements

On the off chance that your video will incorporate designs, title slides, or other mixed media components, you ought to design out things and substance for those pieces before time. These components often consolidated into your storyboards; therefore, the video's material streams flawlessly.

Set the Video Length

As you create your storyboard, you'll additionally get to prefer to what extent your video you need to be. On YouTube, recordings under two minutes get the first significant levels of commitment.

Your video needs to be sufficiently long to convey the key messages that line up with its objective. If you are doing make a more extended video, try various things with how your present substance the pacing, story circular segment, and visuals to stay watchers intrigued throughout.

Pick a Filming Location

You've chosen your video objective, made a storyboard, and chose the perfect video length expected to expire your message. Directly it is a fantastic chance to seek out your shooting territories.

In the film business, this movement is named zone investigating, and like one another development at this time, an enormous little bit of making a persuading video. To start, explore your storyboard and make a summary of the various regions each scene requires. Dependent upon your video thought, you'll simply need one area, but you'll demand another zone for every stage.

Associates, partners, and even family are often fantastic resources here for locating the territories you would like. Recall that for specific areas, almost like associations and other personal property, and you'll require assent from the owner to film. to stay things essential, it's optimal to seek out your regions through people you recognize on any occasion for your underlying, only a few manifestations.

Visit each territory before the shoot. On your investigating trips, guarantee you will have the selection to urge the kinds of shots your requirement for your video.

For the foremost part, it's brighter to possess more room, so you'll change the camera position differing.

You ought to moreover check for any uproarious or encompassing clatters like occupied roads or cooling units that would interfere together with your sound when recording and consider the sunshine and time of day. While space may have adequate light within the initial segment of the day, you'll get to bring a lighting pack in to film during the night or night.

Music and Sound Effects:

Capable quality music and sound impacts can influence a productive video and a bright beginner one. Fortunately, film quality sounds are as of now quickly open, whether or not your chronicles do not have Hollywood-size spending plans.

While picking music for your video, first consider the overall perspective you want to form. Music is one of the foremost noteworthy gadgets for build up the pace of a video and, far of the time, instructs the changing style, camera advancement, and on-camera action. On the off chance that you're familiarizing your picture with another group, you almost certainly got to pick music that's lively and eager.

The second indispensable piece of picking music is gaining the elemental approvals to use the tune.

What you're scanning for here are themes separate as "distinction free." this does not mean the music is going to be free, yet it implies you only remuneration A level rate to use the music and won't need to pay additional powers or allowing costs too.

YouTube features a library of free sound signs and music to use in your accounts. Other mind-blowing resources for sway free music are Pond5, Epidemic Sound, and Premium Beat. The two organizations consolidate numerous expertly recorded and made songs in an immense number of classes at various lengths and beats. Premium Beat and Pond5 both incorporate a vast library of sound impacts to feature surface and significance to your chronicles. Some of the time, it just delivers a shrouded sound outcomes layer far out of a scene to boost the imaginative idea of your video and move your group into the story.

YouTube Marketing Strategy

Since you've delivered a video and advanced it for search, we should always discuss the way to advertise your YouTube channel and recordings. While positioning high in indexed lists and having a vast supporter base is ideal, those objectives are often hard to accomplish when you're only beginning.

That is the rationale. It's essential to repeatedly get the message out about your YouTube channel and recordings across different stages. Luckily, YouTube and different stages make it simple to share video content. The subsequent are a couple of hints for a way to advance your YouTube content on different channels best.

Social Media

Sharing your recordings on social may be a simple method to feature extra bits of data to your video and connect with watchers. YouTube makes it unbelievably straightforward for you et al. to advance your video across other interpersonal organizations. To share a video, simply click the "Offer" tab underneath the video. There you'll choose where to showcase the video. YouTube even gives an abbreviated URL to your video for the helpful posting.

While advancing your YouTube channel or recordings on your online networking destinations, believe the best-promoting procedure. Mostly sharing the video on your course of events or feed might not be the most straightforward alternative. Consider why you made the video. Perhaps you probably did an instructional exercise since clients were posing many inquiries about the way to utilize your item.

It may be ideal for reacting to those inquiries with a connection to your video. On the off chance that you simply made a video as a significant aspect of a much bigger battle or typical pattern, confirm to include essential #hashtags that were proper to ensure your video remember for the discussion. If you made a video to fabricate mindfulness around your image, consider posting the connection in your profile profiles.

Blog Posts and Websites

Market your YouTube channel and recordings on your site and blog. When we are using YouTube follow symbol to your site and blog so your crowd can without much of a stretch discover your channel. Second, implant pertinent recordings on your website or in blog entries. Consider making a YouTube video to travel with a blog entry or sharing client video audits or contextual investigations on your site. Not exclusively will this assistance advertises your YouTube channel and recordings. However, it'll likewise direct people to your site.

To add a YouTube video to your blog or site, duplicate the implant code under the video you would like to spotlight. Check out our bit by bit insert directions here.

Email

While you're on the journey to get and attract new clients and leads, remember about those you as of now have. Offer your video substance and channel with relevant email records. Urge your contacts to seem at a blog entry you've during which inserted a video to increment both the video and site traffic or direct them to a big playlist you've curated. Sending an email pamphlet with essential data and video content is another incredible method to stay your contacts locked in.

Q&A Sites

Do your recordings help lookout of a problem or answer an inquiry? As long as this is often true, captivating with well-known Q&A destinations as Quora could also be a fantastic advertising procedure for your business. Screen questions and offer video content clients will discover supportive.

Collaborate with others

Does your organization have a relationship with another organization that has an unprecedented YouTube nearness? Request that they work together! Working alongside others is a pleasant path for the two channels to select up a presentation to a different crowd. Make a video or playlist together.

There are many alternatives to team with different brands inventively; simply make sure that their group and objective is like yours. The association needs to line up together with your showcasing procedure.

Engage with viewers

At long last, confirm to attract together with your watchers. React to remarks, answer questions, request criticism, and thank watchers for his or her help. It is often an easy undertaking to overlook or let fall by the wayside, so plan to pick a committed time to see video collaborations and react to clients.

YouTube Analytics

First, you cannot gauge your prosperity without deciding your objective. If you've recorded, altered, transferred, streamlined, and shared your video and still do not have the foggiest idea what purpose you're attempting to accomplish, we have got a problem. Your objective should drive your video technique from start to end.

You should consider that specialize in one objective for every video (as we mention here).

The most common video objectives are to expand brand mindfulness, perspectives, clicks, or inbound connections or social offers.

Contingent upon how you utilize the video in your showcasing material, the target might be to create the open pace of an email arrangement or improve the change rate on the purpose of arrival. YouTube is a fantastic stage for developing brand mindfulness.

As the world's second-biggest web index, YouTube permits your recordings to be seen through natural pursuit or paid to market. Video is a unique method to adapt your image by displaying genuine workers, clients, or accomplices. It additionally permits you to fabricate believability by distributing educational substance that helps your objective purchaser. Advancing your recordings through paid publicizing versus natural pursuit can affect the type of video you need to make. Just in case you mean to build mindfulness naturally, belief shooting the historical backdrop of your organization, client surveys, or item instructional exercises.

Key Matrix's

Since we've discussed why deciding an objective is so significant, we will mention the way to quantify achievement viably. From the beginning, YouTube investigation is often quite overpowering.

On the opposite side, it's disappointing once you post a video and do not get an equivalent number of perspectives or the maximum amount of commitment as you were anticipating. YouTube investigation gives you ways watchers discovered your substance, to what extent they watched it, and therefore the amount they drew in with it. How about we start by going once more what precisely you'll quantify and the way to get it.

To start with, head to youtube.com/investigation. You need to coordinate with an investigation dashboard that shows an overview of how your recordings are performing during the previous 28 days. You'll change the investigation period by tapping on the menu within the upper right-hand corner. The diagram report includes some top-line execution measurements, commitment measurements, socioeconomics, traffic sources, and mainstream content.

You can likewise channel your outcomes by content, gadget type, geology or area, all video substance or playlists, supporter status, playback type, traffic by various YouTube items, and interpretations. Notwithstanding sifting outcomes, YouTube permits you to point out your leads to a good range of graphs and even a quick guide.

Watch Time and Audience

Watch time reports the whole number of minutes your crowd has spent survey your substance on your channel beat all and by video. It causes you to ascertain what bits of substance watchers are really expending instead of merely tapping on and exploring endlessly since.

Watch time is critical because it's one of YouTube's positioning elements. A video with a better watch time is sure to rank higher in results. YouTube gives a detail report on watch time, sees, average view length, and average rate saw for singular recordings, area, distribute date, and that is only the tip of the iceberg.

A video's standard rate saw, or degree of consistency, shows the average level of a video your crowd watches per see. A better rate implies there is a higher possibility that your group will watch that video until the top. Take a stab at putting cards and end screens in recordings with a better average rate saw rate to enhance the number of perspectives your suggestions to get the act.

Traffic

The traffic sources report shows how watchers are finding your substance on the online. It provides significant knowledge about where to advance your YouTube content best.

As an example, you'll check whether watchers are finding your material through YouTube search or Twitter. To ascertain more inside and out traffic revealing, click on the overall traffic source classification. This information can help refine your YouTube promoting system. Confirm to upgrade your metadata hooked into your discoveries.

Demographics

The socioeconomics report encourages you to grasp your crowd by covering their age and sex. You'd then be ready to separate age gatherings and sexual orientations by other criteria, for instance, geology. This report will assist you with bettering the business to your YouTube crowd and comprehend if your substance is resounding together with your found-out purchaser personas.

Engagement Reports

Commitment reports assist you in realizing what substance is reverberating together with your crowd. Here you'll perceive what watchers are clicking, sharing, remarking, and advancing. You'll likewise observe how your cards and end screens are acting in your commitment reports. Cards and end screens reports assist you to realize what your crowd is connecting with, so you'll upgrade your invitations to figure in future recordings.

Now Set and Action

With quite a billion dynamic clients, YouTube can't get home for original recordings anymore. Video drives a 157% expansion in natural hour gridlock from web indexes. YouTube may be a sound advertising stage that furnishes your image with the prospect to advance substance during a visual and connecting way.

It's essential to rehearse inbound showcasing methods when promoting your YouTube channel and recordings. Make content that shares a charming story and furnishes your watchers with crucial data. A market that content across various stages, including social, email, and organization blog or site. Improve your substance by including cards and end screens with clear CTAs.

YouTube may appear to be overpowering from the outset, yet the stage makes it very simple to share and review content. Your crowd must learn, be engaged, and attract together with your image through video, so confirm to follow this manual to form the foremost out of your YouTube showcasing procedure.

Chapter 6: Twitter

An all-around created procedure is the establishment for progress, and it's what isolates the best brands on Twitter from the additionally ran. Without a reasonable arrangement, you will sit around idly and cash tweeting without an away from how your exercises are helping your association meet its objectives. What's more, when it comes time to audit your presentation, you'll battle to demonstrate what you've accomplished. What's more, that will make it difficult to put forth the defence for expanding your group size or spending plan.

Consistently you spend on research and procedure will take care often. We guarantee. It is what you must do:

Define success and set goals

All right, so you have an intelligent response prepared when your manager asks, "For what reason would we say we are on Twitter?" Then come the two follow-up punches: "Would we say we are on target to meet our objectives? What's more, what are they once more?"

Addressing these inquiries isn't hard if you get your work done. Start with a rundown of your association's present elevated level business targets, for example,

- Create leads and deals
- Increment client devotion
- Construct brand and item mindfulness
- Lessening client assistance costs

From these destinations, make explicit and quantifiable objectives. It will make it simple for you to assess advance and demonstrate achievement. For instance, if your goal is to furnish your business group with top-notch leads through social, your objective may be "use Twitter to drive 30 email recruits for every month."

With targets and objectives set up, make sure to set aside some effort to benchmark the present condition of your group's presentation. It will assist you with estimating your advancement toward your objectives, demonstrating that your methodology is delivering genuine, quantifiable outcomes for your business.

Characterizing and estimating accomplishment via web-based networking media can be testing, so setting aside the effort to do this correctly will genuinely separate you. Our manual for the ROI of web-based life separates the procedure for you.

Competition of research

Get-together data about your rivals' qualities and shortcomings on social is primary. Not sure where to begin? Peruse our snappy guide, and afterwards utilize this serious investigation format to structure a common showcasing technique that will leave your rivals in the residue.

Identify the target audience

Your image can't be everything to all individuals on Twitter, nor should you need it to be. Realize whom you're focusing on and create a methodology that centres around conveying a genuine incentive to them. It will urge them to draw in with your image and, in the end, become clients and backers. While you're busy, look at our guide on the most proficient method to pull in and connect more Twitter devotees.

Audit your account

Contingent upon the size of your organization and your objectives, you might need to utilize a separate Twitter account or numerous records for various divisions or capacities. If multiple individuals in your association are, as of now, using Twitter, evaluating and combining existing files is vital.

Integration of twitter with the whole society

How significant is this? At the point when the Vancouver Canucks hockey group erased rebel accounts and propelled official internet-based life channels as a component of their social methodology, they had the option to develop their Twitter fan base by 800 per cent deliberately.

Groups working in huge (or developing) associations can wind up working in storehouses. If you discover this incident to your showcasing social group, ensure you hold tearing down those storehouses, and remain associated with different groups. Their work can be a rich wellspring of data and resources for share with your devotees. Furthermore, they might be gathering bits of knowledge that can open new open doors for your Twitter system.

Keep your account unique

While it's conceivable and straightforward to present a similar substance to various informal organizations, cross-posting isn't a methodology we suggest.

Each system has its one of a kind qualities and client base, so while applying a similar procedure to different systems may appear to be an alternate route, it may cost you more in commitment and genuineness than it spares you in time and exertion.

Nail your technique on each system in turn, keeping it one of a kind and new

Chapter 7: LinkedIn

This section investigates LinkedIn and discusses how it very well may be consolidated into a web-based social networking advertising system, including taking a gander at LinkedIn pages, which can create for an organization or a person. We likewise contacted on LinkedIn gatherings and spread LinkedIn's expanding alternatives for publicizing.

LinkedIn Do's and Don'ts

With everything taken into account, developing a closeness on LinkedIn is probably commonly significant to a B2B (business-to-business) association, where your customers are different associations or affiliations, including people who are potentially bound to put vitality in LinkedIn. As an electronic life promoter, the need might be for you to strengthen your profile on LinkedIn. For example, you can make a LinkedIn social event, and it might be a course for people to look at a subject. To develop a framework for searching for a business or clients, you may need to search for and join LinkedIn social events and work on including cases of adventures you to do to become your LinkedIn portfolio.

The proposed fundamental for considering LinkedIn as a web-based life channel is to begin fortifying your pith at first. Not solely will it help you with your work, be that as it may, on the off chance that you do end up getting remembered for working up proximity on LinkedIn for a client, people will without a doubt take a gander at your profile, fundamentally if you make or team up in LinkedIn get-togethers. My general, strong proposal is to research LinkedIn. Perhaps set aside a half-hour at any rate once consistently to look at your profile. Create it a piece and get inclined to get required on LinkedIn. Work toward considering LinkedIn right when you make another endeavour or work on one and introducing the results on your profile.

To the extent general web-based systems administration promoting, I moreover endorse getting at any rate somewhat familiar with the options LinkedIn has for B2B internet organizing, tallying how an association/affiliation page can be made, similarly as taking a gander at a bit of the publicizing choices LinkedIn has.

It's not cautiously B2B (business to business), the same number of associations more, affiliations that have most likely some LinkedIn page proximity, whether or not it's uninvolved.

Dynamically, in any event, when everything said in done and "B2C" (business to the purchaser) conditions, LinkedIn is used for selecting, posting vocations. It's a brilliant idea to get familiar with it. Whether or not you're in a vast affiliation, don't "expect" anyone is regulating LinkedIn. As a web-based systems administration publicist, you may have the alternative to examine how it will, in general, used. Correspondingly, similarly, as with various channels, I trust it's fundamental to consider ROI. With LinkedIn explicitly, it has become a default community point for associations, non-benefits, and pretty much any business searcher, so at any rate, your affiliation should have a page. Furthermore, someone guaranteeing the information is exact. They should post sometimes, or if nothing else, posting businesses, openings, adventures. The noteworthiness of this augmentations multiple times if your chief or client is a B2B substance, where people may discover you on LinkedIn as an association. It's moreover apparent that right when people search on Google, it might turn up the association or affiliation page. It's a savvy thought to keep an eye out for it and possibly impact it. For example, here's an instance of a notable association and its LinkedIn page:

Understanding LinkedIn

LinkedIn grasps the best movement is to utilize it routinely. On the off chance that for a couple of reasons, you don't have a LinkedIn account, I vivaciously propose you get one.

If you have one yet don't have many "affiliations," I invite you to go on to a spot like Vista Print, go for the free business cards (where you pay for "sending just"), and consider making a business card with necessary contact information, including your LinkedIn Profile interface.

The clarification I propose a direct business card (whether or not you have an "official" one) is to just have some around, with the objective that when you think about it, you can get in the affinity for inviting people to connect with you on LinkedIn.

You'll in like manner need to begin inviting people by email, for instance, partners occupied with working, or clients, or graduate class in case you went to a college. Try not to disregard relatives, neighbours, additionally, people you see each week.

The general advantage of taking a pinch of time and broadening your framework on LinkedIn is that it will, in general, be a helpful, fundamental gadget for a partner with jobs and new clients.

For example, you should contact someone to get some data about a particular endeavour, work. Even though you presumably won't know them before long, someone you know does, as ought to be apparent from LinkedIn. LinkedIn urges you to connect with people, which, for sure, people, has an even more surprising, viable impact than Facebook in setting up frameworks. However, don't be unobtrusive on the off chance that you've never endeavoured it!

Creating a LinkedIn Page:

Making a LinkedIn page anticipates that you should take care of certain obligations. Abhorrence making a discretionary site, and it genuinely should be credible.

On the off chance that you're learning web-based life-advancing, I recommend thinking about making a website for yourself, with an "official" webpage name, for instance, blahsocial.com/net/and getting an "official" email address (you@blahsocial.com). Somewhat, this will be helpful as a movement in learning bit by bit guidelines to set up an Internet closeness, period. To do this, I endorse examining the most practical site plans at places like godaddy.com and 1and1.com, and making notes, in any occasion, calling up, besides, speaking with a live individual, about the most affordable way to deal with make a site with your name.

If you have to endeavour the Google course and have the most affordable month to month cost, you can a portion of the time register the site name, (for instance, blahsocial.com), which fuses email capacity, and not use godaddy.com or 1and1.com for encouraging the site. Instead, you can point the site name at free help, for instance, Google Sites.

I also recommend looking at strikingly.com, Wix, Weebly, and Shopify and essentially giving them a shot.

After you've endeavoured all the free ones, pick one for your "official" site.

It's worthy of getting settled with them all if a client needs help with working up Internet proximity. If you're used by a progressively conspicuous association, it can at present end up being helpful to realize how to make a microsite reliant on a particular campaign. You can start by glancing through this territory to appreciate when everything is said in done what you should do to make a LinkedIn page. At the point when you have your official site and a conventional email, return and have a go at making a LinkedIn page.

https://www.linkedin.com/organization/include/appear

Interesting Thing:

One of the exciting things to me is that a gadget like Hootsuite, which we'll look at in a later part, licenses you to introduce simultaneously on various frameworks. I worked at a B2B startup, and they expected to secure over various electronic life channels viably. I would make a blog section, which was the central, official spot for new substances. By then, using Hootsuite, I subsequently introduced on Facebook, Twitter, and LinkedIn. By LinkedIn, it wasn't that there must be much work put into it, in any case, when the right pieces were set up, it was commonly easy to introduce substance on it.

ROI Strategies for LinkedIn

So how might you figure ROI on LinkedIn?

In case you created aficionados, you may post offers/deals now and again, and you could speculatively follow what occurred.

Another sensible technique to consider LinkedIn is as an outlet for PR, or on the other hand, only one more way to deal with produce trustworthiness with material substance.

It is exceptionally substantial in a B2B setting, where making material and sharing it employing electronic systems administration media can be a way to deal with help people with getting some answers concerning appropriate subjects and lift legitimacy.

LinkedIn in like manner needs to advance, and on occasion, especially in a B2B setting, the general cost of a thing or organization might be higher. I'm not following or separating the focal points of cost; in any case, when everything is said in done, LinkedIn commercials could end up being more excessive than general declarations on Facebook or Google. It is because it is incredibly drawn in the business swarm. Since you may stay to secure from a valuable arrangement in a B2B setting, there are more longing for in that setting to pay for the notices. As a learning experience, have a go at making promotions on LinkedIn:

https://business.linkedin.com/

At that point, investigate the showcasing side:

https://business.linkedin.com/showcasingarran gements

Conclusion:

An obligation of appreciation is for examining! LinkedIn is a noteworthy device for online life publicists, meaning structure your quality and perceiving how to set an association or relationship up with its page. If you intend to do autonomous, this can in like manner be assistance. Something that may be ignored or something you could achieve for a local business or relationship to get understanding.

You may, in like manner, need to examine for other online life discussion bundles on LinkedIn. It might be an acceptable distinguishing proof on your profile and a way to deal with get some answers concerning new things.

Chapter 8: Hootsuite

Online life by assisting in making and introducing content on various casual associations. It's a bit of the "skill toolbox" that I endorse exploring. In case you haven't made a blog, Facebook page, Twitter record, and LinkedIn page yet, I endorse keeping an eye on the main parts at present, making those records. You can get something out of this part necessarily by minding it, yet I recommend establishing up those precedents and after that "interfacing" them to Hootsuite. The LinkedIn page isn't cautiously essential, yet I propose characterizing the goal of having 2-3 web-based life records to post. I in like manner prescribe considering your blog as an "order post" for online life, the central spot where you make and distribute content from the outset, which you by then post to various electronic life properties. Some part of the clarification behind this is because, with a blog, it's really "your" relational association. But on the off chance that Google or WordPress goes down ablaze, your blog will be around for whatever period that you need it, and you control it.

You could battle the identical for Facebook and Twitter and LinkedIn at any rate concerning the likelihood of them continuing, in any case, the focal job of a blog is substance, and you have significantly higher authority over things. At any cost, in case everything sounds unnecessarily applied, the perfect way to deal with giving things a shot can't merely to develop a long electric range interpersonal communication closeness, in any case, to make one and see what happens when you post content on a nonstop reason. By then, you'll start to see the satisfaction and enthusiasm when people comment on your blog passage, as your post on Facebook, get more supporters on Twitter. You may also encounter what numerous people have encountered an ejection of starting fervour, brave targets, and a short time later getting involved (or overwhelmed) with the goal that the aggregate and consistency of substance stream off. (I'm culpable of this myself!

Do whatever it takes not to solicit me what number from online diaries or destinations I have!)

It is the explanation after some time, and I've would, by and large, slant toward free gadgets.

With paid site accounts, it might look increasingly incredible, however at this point and once more, reasonability is vast than looking cute. It's more brilliant to have a free site you don't have to pay for, than the one you have to fight with and finish up whether to pay for on an advancing reason. I'm on a fundamental level talking about individual goals since when you get into business or non-advantage regions, it probably looks good to have the most master site you can. Regardless, I, for the most part, propose contemplating what is viable. Since online life is, as I might want to accept, necessarily about substance sharing time, I believe it's necessary to consider what is sensible to the extent time spent, furthermore, level of gainfulness, from the soonest beginning stage. At the inside, anything that makes it less challenging to make and post content is something to be grateful. It is the explanation Google's instruments are satisfactory because you contribute less vitality and trouble fiddling around and can focus on the substance. Hootsuite fits legitimately in the focal point of that. Right when you develop the substance, Hootsuite helps make it trouble-free and direct to introduce substance on various frameworks, including booking things early.

It's not fundamental to see the total of the other options.

(Remember, in an earlier area, the discussion about picking some "potential" things focusing on learning a couple of fundamentals with the objective that you don't get overwhelmed.)

The Plans and Pricing join justifies looking at, and it's charming to know there's a free structure. At the point when everything is said in done, the gadget turns around managing the creation and posting of substance. It can similarly be used for social tuning in, which urges you to get a sentiment of what people are expressing about you on your online life goals.

ROI Strategies

Hootsuite joins assessment and impelled checking capacities. You can utilize Hootsuite to check the pace of gainfulness, yet that, finally, relies upon how you measure ROI. I doubtlessly think it justifies getting some answers concerning, even even though it seems like ROI can be somewhat, soft.

Eventually, I trust it's very beneficial to express that

Hootsuite and ROI most likely partner when you develop an ordinary stream of substance about your business or affiliation that passes on appropriate information about the things, activities, or the other hand heritage — fundamentally the "story" of your affiliation.

This invaluable substance, which can in like manner be posted on an official website or blog, not merely helps with webpage improvement (getting situated well in Google list things), yet it moreover makes people go to your webpage. It's the perfect substance for business. The ROI is building a base of information about the association, the site improvement regard. (It can bolster bargains in the condition you're selling something, so you can connect SEO to profit.) The substance is steadfast, and Hootsuite makes you share it with your casual associations. In any case, there are some various ways to deal with look at ROI, and I recommend taking two or three minutes to look through these blog sections. They will give you a sentiment of the sorts of things people are doing, and the language they use around ROI likewise, web-based life:

- http://blog.hootsuite.com/build-andmeasure-social-media-roi/
- http://blog.hootsuite.com/webtrends/
- http://blog.hootsuite.com/measure-socialmedia-roi-business/
- http://blog.hootsuite.com/8-tips-forsocial-business-7/
- http://blog.hootsuite.com/social-media-roiintroduction/
- http://blog.hootsuite.com/webinar-contentconverting-social-media-roi/

To gain hero internet based life great focuses, I enthusiastically suggest getting into the inclination for doing Google look on topics like "return for capital contributed and .." (you fill in the casual association or gadget). On the off chance that you will pardon one Star Wars reference at present, request you for the sake of Obi-Wan Kenobi to endeavour Google check out ROI and instruments. Examine the articles and blog sections. People share their experiences, benchmarks, and best practices. (Besides, push knock, you can blog about this too! The more examination of ROI, the better, whether or not you're merely elucidating what you don't have the foggiest thought. Without a doubt, even that can be valuable and encouraging to other people, who are out there doing kind of Google look likewise.)

Conclusion

An obligation of appreciation is for scrutinizing this part. I think Hootsuite is a tolerable instrument for web-based life promoters to use. It's a central thing in your apparatus stash. As strong as it seems to be, it doesn't make the substance for you, so to a great extent, I accept that Chapter 2 is the most noteworthy area of all. In any case, whatever makes it more straightforward for you to work with content spares your chance to develop the substance.

Chapter 9: Snapchat

Advertising your business on Snapchat isn't for each organization. We're not proposing that you join without a procedure, comprehension of its client base, and in particular, a promise to making content that might be not quite the same as anything you've made previously. That is the primary thing you must comprehend: This online networking stage doesn't care for some other stage out there. It's about customized informing, ongoing video, emoticons, and doodles, and eccentric substance. It's crude and loaded with character. Brand telling that feels too proficient is viewed as exhausting on the application. In case you're not ready to consider some fresh possibilities, try and have some good times, at that point, it's not the correct web-based life advertising stage for you at any rate not at present.

So, for what reason would you need to advertise your organization on Snapchat?

There is rivalry, and in this manner, you're bound to stick out.

There's likewise no calculation concealing your posts.

In the off chance, when the client includes your business as a companion, they can see many things without much stretch and see that you've added a Story and play it. Ultimately, there are scarcely any advertisements and no connections to drive traffic away from seeing and associating with your substance.

On the off chance that your organization's energetic about the benefit of building brand mindfulness through Snapchat, the initial steps are to make a record, acclimate yourself with the interface, and set up your profile.

Snapchat Marketing

Snapchat's client base slants youthful: 71% of all clients are younger than 34-years of age. So, in case you're hoping to associate with and make more brand advocates among that age gathering, Snapchat is an incredible spot to be. It likewise implies you must painstakingly consider the sort of substance your young crowd needs that begins with a solid comprehension of who your purchaser personas are and what they need from you.

Figure out how to utilize purchaser persona formats for composing your crowd fragments and making your showcasing more grounded.

Purchaser personas are fictionalized adaptations of your optimal client. To make a persona, you pull certain information about the practices and reactions of your present and past client base, posing inquiries, for example, what makes a client bound to purchase? What are the methods of my "best" clients (the individuals who are generally faithful or have the most elevated lifetime esteem)?

You direct statistical surveying and meetings to figure out what the segment subtleties, sparks, and objectives of your optimal purchaser. This data is then blended into a depiction of an anecdotal purchaser who will fill in as a token of your intended interest group when drafting advertising materials and advancements and building up informing.

Knowing the crowd cosmetics of Snapchat, you might need to return to your examination and decide whether there were various propensities and objectives of those younger than 34.

You could likewise lead a little centre gathering by a talk with a portion of your best clients who are eager Snapchat clients to figure out what they search for in a brand, how regularly they utilize the application, how to communicate with their companions on the form, and what they might want to see from you.

It will give you an incredible beginning stage for understanding who you are speaking with and fitting your advertising endeavours on the scene.

Behind the scenes

On Snapchat, individuals lean toward the unpolished, legitimate look. In the background, visits and sneak tops at new items permit your crowd to feel increasingly associated and a piece of the experience.

Interactive projects

Get your crowd snapping by doing exercises. They can take an interest. The underneath Story from Starbucks (@starbucks) highlights a picture they need individuals to attract on and send to their companions an extraordinary case of a brand considering the stage's local highlights and utilizing this to drive a commendable offer battle.

Takeovers

Worker takeovers assist individuals with becoming more acquainted with your colleagues and see what life at your organization resembles. It's an enjoyable approach to feature your way of life, the interests of your staff individuals, and get a new and fascinating substance that is outside the domain of your office and items.

Users generated campaigns

Curating Snaps, including your crowd, can push the prominence of your record. Ask your clients, group on other social stages, and Snapchat companions to send you Snaps you can highlight in an up and coming Story on a subject. You could likewise attach this to a giveaway to produce extra intrigue and entries.

How-to videos

The Story design loans itself well to showing somebody how to accomplish something so, instructional recordings. Ask your agents what inquiries they as often as possible get asked or look at the most mainstream look on your site. Consider who in your group has a fascinating ability and grandstand this with regards to a Story. It doesn't need to be that genuine. Taco Bell (@tacobell) distributed a Story itemizing the battles of opening a sauce parcel and some capricious and insufficient approaches.

Interviews with seniors

Use Snapchat to give your organization's senior initiative group a stage where they can talk legitimately to clients and possibilities, give their suppositions, and feature what's next for your organization that gets them energized.

This kind of access to a portion of your colleagues may happen a couple of times each year, if not less, relying upon the size of your association and customer base. It encourages individuals to become more acquainted with your organization's administrators better, which can go far when expanding trust and regard for your business.

Games

A game can be an enjoyable approach to get your crowd communicating with you on Snapchat either through the talk highlight or by requesting that your congregation send you Snaps. You could even component these in your Story that day.

Commentary on news

The incredible thing about Snapchat is that it is anything but difficult to make a short video and rapidly get it before your crowd there's no requirement for stressing over lighting, arrangement, or altering. When something newsworthy occurs, get an inward master on camera to clarify the occasion, its suggestions, or what they find intriguing about the news. You can likewise survey various individuals in your office to hear a couple of fleeting thoughts and responses. It is a fundamental and connecting approach to give an essential and fascinating substance.

Chapter 10: Social Media Marketing and Analytics

This segment looks at the demonstration of online life watching, which is too known as social tuning. It's a noteworthy bit of electronic long-range interpersonal communication advancing. We'll similarly explore social assessment, which can help you with seeing how your web-based social networking attempts are going. We'll look at a couple of related gadgets and give things a shot.

Social Media Marketing, Listening and Analytics

A monstrous bit of web-based life promoting is beginning conversations and putting content on casual associations, one more essential piece of it is checking out what people are expressing. For example, after erstwhile, one way to deal with see how convincing your undertakings are is to comprehend what people are stating about them either through direct responses or on their online life accounts.

On a fundamental level, you could scrutinize each post, notwithstanding, how might you find them? What do you do if there are a vast amount of posts? Mechanical assemblies have created to help you with seeing how things are going.

Internet-based life checking is the way toward distinguishing and figuring out what is being said about a brand, individual, or item through various social and online channels. Like web indexes that send crawlers to the most distant ranges of the Internet, web-based life checking is a calculation-based apparatus that creeps' locales and persistently records them. When destinations are listed, they can be looked through dependent on inquiries or strings. Most checking instruments work by sneaking locales ceaselessly and ordering them. Some are crept continuously, for example, Twitter. Different areas may be slithered less frequently – state, at regular intervals, or consistently, on the off chance that they are less significant. A few apparatuses, like us, do this slithering themselves. Others use information suppliers. We'll let you surmise which of those alternatives we believe is better.

Anyhow, when each one of those locales is recorded, they would then be able to be looked at Most instruments utilize some type of questions or search strings that the client writes to discover notices of explicit words and expressions on those pages. It will, at that point, bring these (we call them 'specifies') over into the instrument's interface, which would then be able to be perused, cut, diced.

Web-based life Monitoring is regularly mistaken for different terms like Social Media Listening or Social Media Intelligence, yet, every one of these monikers has its place in your social examination tool kit.

Online life Intelligence is an overall term covering a couple of crucial territories of social examination, including Social Media Monitoring and Social Media Listening, with an emphasis on Competitor Analysis. It speaks to the entirety of the parts (i.e., information) these different instruments open.

Online networking Listening reveals purchaser bits of knowledge you can apply to mark procedure. It's a continuous undertaking that centers around becoming acquainted with your crowd and their feelings, so you have a benchmark comprehension of the purchasers you need your image to reach. The objective is to realize that the buyers generally care about and the main things into your client involvement era.

Online networking Monitoring is additionally a progressing try, yet with a marginally unique core interest. If you consider Social Media Listening as making a benchmark for what your crowd feels, Social Media Monitoring is about the upkeep of that pattern.

Write Unique Content:

With the billions of online networking clients around the world, doubtlessly that probably a portion of your adherents or the individuals perusing your profile — have additionally observed your rival's substance or that of different organizations in your industry. That is the reason you should have connecting with online networking content that sticks out and furnishes watchers with motivation to click that "Follow" fasten and interface with your image.

To assist you with getting imaginative, consider the substance your rivals are sharing and how you can extraordinarily advance your items. Likewise, exploit the highlights offered by the stage you're utilizing. For instance, you can make live recordings on Facebook to share the most recent insights concerning an item dispatch or lead a giveaway.

In conclusion, utilize your present clients and advertisers to assist you with producing content. You can do this by re-posting their substance or urging them to utilize a hashtag to impart their own encounters and pictures to your items (like Frye's Instagram hashtag that I referenced before).

Negative Sentiment Gets Lots of Attention

How about we take a gander at the negative side of the condition first, since social antagonism is so harming when it turns into a web sensation. There are three critical things you're searching for in your checking:

1. At the point when purchasers negatively talk about your image via web-based networking media, they're likely not by any means the only clients who feel that way. Here are some educational insights to remember:

2. Just 1 of every 26 troubled clients will whine to you; of the non-grumblers, 91% simply leave. It makes it even more critical to deal with the individuals who do whine – to give perceivably to the ones who are quietly viewing. On the off chance that they see you dealing with the others, they may give you another possibility. Be that as it may, you can't deal with client objections except if you think about them.

3. Americans inform more individuals regarding terrible encounters (15 individuals overall) than about great ones (11 individuals by and large). The issue is, despairing people tend to be desperate for kindred spirits. Those 15 individuals may be glad to share a social post about a terrible encounter on the off chance that they've persevered through

comparative. Any uptick in the negative notion is unquestionably caused for concern.

4. Then again, when client administration issues are settled well, 70% of some time ago, disappointed clients will give marks another opportunity. It is the reason the speed and exactness AI Analytics brings to the table is urgent.

Alerting You to Crises Before They Spiral

The excellence of Social Media Monitoring apparatuses – the best ones, in any event, is you can set up alarms so you realize when there's a spike in slant demonstrating a subject or post you shouldn't overlook. That way, you can address issues rapidly and prevent irate posts from turning into a web sensation.

These alarms use catchphrases you pick, just as a measurement called Passion Intensity that tells you the quality of feelings in social posts. At the point when Passion Intensity spikes, it's an excellent opportunity to examine why.

This careful consideration is the thing that permits brands like Buffalo Wild Wings to follow the notion around a possibly hazardous crusade pumpkin zest seasoned wing sauce.

Listening

One common distortion is the conviction that social tuning in and social watching is something fundamentally the same as in replaceable terms for one method. In truth, a social change in and social watching, anything regularly used together have prominent occupations to do, much like your CEO and CFO.

Social checking is connected to seeing or being caused mindful of certain primary events as they to happen; for instance, a customer fight getting much thought. It's setting up a benchmark and watching for when things go wrong from it, using social checking out get why. What, by then, is social tuning? Furthermore, how achieves social listening work?

This article will react to that question in detail, with explicit respect for its multifaceted limits (which you can click ahead to, dependent upon your prerequisites), including:

- For what reason is social listening noteworthy?
- Comprehend end to follow brand prosperity
- Recognize and improve substance to meet your dedication destinations
- Configuration fights that will win from the beginning

- Make a genuine, altered association with each touchpoint
- Consider and dispatch new things to a horde of individuals arranged to treasure them

Social listening works identified with social seeing to give an as a rule and all-the-time measure for your picture to work. It's an organized examination of your group, what they care about, and where they look at such things. It's connected to uncovering and conglomerating all the information you're missing if you simply count likes and takes note.

Social listening researches the general social scene taking in the regular shapes and sounds, so variations from the norm become more straightforward to spot.

Importance

Watching is a noteworthy safety measure, yet nothing beats a dependable, proactive system. Much equivalent to a powerful, safe system is necessary to shield the body from being enthusiastically helpless against sickness, and social listening keeps your picture aware of the end-all strategy.

Instead of focusing on single tweets and issues, you get a collected view that highlights examples and subjects you can use to organize brand strategies.

Not under any condition like social watching, making you mindful of a single issue that you handle at the time social listening sparks a light on nonstop points. Perhaps you have a similar issue jumping up by and substantial around a similar time, or in a particular geographical zone. Instead of offering a helpful answer to satisfy a lone customer, you can deal with the issue at the root and get rid of it proceeding.

In any case, it's not just about handling issues. Social listening offers information you can apply to any piece of brand exercises.

Engagement with optimized content

The social substance isn't just about "being on social." Content is essential to responsibility and change, so you have to put everything in order. It is the spot social listening devices like Net Base come into accommodating because they clear out much experimentation.

Taking a gander at your picture gives you which substance is resounding and on which channels. That urges you to design the sort of substance you need.

We should imagine you've comprehended an enormous bit of your dedication is on Instagram, so you understand that visual substance is commonly massive.

Or then again, if destinations are getting you the most balanced, you understand the content is your group's tendency.

That is the spot supposition returns. You can look at hashtags, topics, and watchwords to see what people talk about most vivaciously, and how that relates to the substance, they team up with and share. It furthermore urges you to progress for search.

Or then again, you can hope to Net Base's first-to-feature human-made thinking stage, AI Studio, which therefore discovers subjects for you, considering numerous data centers emerging from point conversations you have to appreciate. It improves listening tries radically, isolated. Likewise, it can help you with recognizing hashtags; you may have missed something different.

Instagram is very hashtag arranged, so knowing which hashtags are notable and noteworthy to your subject area is essential. On various channels, you'll move the inside to the ideal catchphrases/terms.

The terms people use while searching for whatever your picture offers are enormous.

Thus AI-controlled the automated divulgence is a certified preferred position.

The specific inverse thing you need is one of your opponent's discovering this hashtag and making it their own before you do! Coming up first in hashtag question things can be a considerable brand care help.

Nevertheless, what do you do once you understand where to find your group? How might you interface really with them? That is the spot the real force of social listening comes in, as it makes you adjust your picture.

Designs Campaign:

The greatness of social listening is that information you accumulate from one district like substance spills into others. Content is the establishment of restricted time fights, yet that is apparently, not by any means the only idea.

Social listening is something you have to apply to your entire order, not only your picture. Right when you do, you will spot designs you can use in different habits – like promotion campaigns.

What does your group need, and by what means may you use those bits of information? Would it be prudent for you to run a test? Offer a one of a kind? Solicitation customer delivered content. Your social listening will tell you.

Also, this is the spot constantly genuinely helps as well. You must acknowledge what your group is into NOW.

You furthermore need to separate influencers yet be sure they're helping keep the conversation positive. Additionally, that they're describing to a story that will bolster you, subsequently, share winning comprehension with primary accomplices and brand underpins (expecting you have those likewise, a similar number of doing!). Shows and difficulties offer arranged occasions of this.

Convince and launch new products

With pressed markets, propelled shopping outperforming coming up, and other present-day brand challenges, most brands can't remain to bomb when they dispatch new things and organizations. Social listening is reliably on the investigation that lets you find what features and articles your group needs and which they eventually don't.

You may even find a unique idea for a brand association.

Pamela Mittoo, Manager of Technical Consumer Research at The Coca-Cola Company, united with Anupam Singh, prime supporter of 113 Industries, a client investigates the association, for the thing, headway works out.

Social listening helped Coke recognize another boondock of business and thing progression by checking out what clients were expressing employing online systems administration media. As Anupam explains, the Net Base stage gives their gatherings an increasingly significant examination of social assessment, constrained by electronic thinking, which empowers brands to discover what clients hurt for and recognize basic practices in the sustenance and refreshment industry.

Besides, those practices are being shared about everything in every vertical, and they're all online at present. Using an instrument prepared to harness and separate sorted out, and unstructured data at scale is the primary differentiator for these noteworthy players. Besides, it very well perhaps for your picture as well!

Social Media Crisis

As I keep an eye out in the space of online life-promoting, I acknowledge that checking for crisis conditions can be one of the most practical ways to deal with use web-based life. (This is despite considering your appearance on the hypothesis to follow when social produces pay.)

Once in awhile, it's a powerless side. Until you have a promoting crisis, it's difficult to escape from how costly one can be. Be that as it may, it will, in general, be an impressive course of action and can cause essential cash identified with hurt for any business. It can cost numerous dollars to "clean up" a publicizing crisis, and for humbler associations, while the dollar aggregates may not be as extraordinary, it can influence being helpful or not.

The essential clarification it's an amazingly massive issue in electronic life exhibiting is since online nearness licenses messages to spread so quickly. I was at a social affair about online nearness. A representative from a significant PR firm was discussing PR crises, and how the time you have to respond to an emergency before it increases out of intensity has decreased. Presently, it's faulty that it will, in general, involve hours before something horrendous gets national media thought.

For example, consider what happened to Target in 2013. It had a "data crack" (which, adventitiously, can happen to any business).

Basic Social Analytics

A social examination can be a focal locale, or even a gave activity.

There has been growing excitement for it, and new gadgets turning out because there is an example toward associations expecting to follow the ROI of their web-based life tries (stun). Once in a while, this infers assessing models, for instance, extension and advancement in internet organizing properties, or choosing whether the conversation around a particular association or fight is specific or negative. Maybe the least requesting ways to deal with see social examination, all things considered, is to go to a Facebook page you made and click on the Insights associate:

ROI Strategies

Social perception is on the soft side of web-based life, in that there aren't various gadgets that join a superb technique to comprehend the budgetary impact of duty or course idea. It is fragmented because, except if a social checking or examination gadget is connected directly to web business, where you can follow the money related impact, it's hard or hard to measure the ROI.

Regardless, for purposes, for instance, checking for the potential crises, and get a sentiment of what people are talking about, it is precious.

A couple of associations copy through the vast majority of their undertakings tuning in for conversations in which someone is whimpering about a thing or has a request, with the objective that customer help can respond quickly and honestly utilizing electronic systems administration media.

My general proposal when pondering using social checking for affiliation or client is to focus on crisis watch. Make a crisis course of action; additionally, do some consistent checking for customer care issues (no business is absurdly little for this, even secretly run associations). The social review can moreover be utilized to get a sentiment of how people react to another fight.

You are building an after on Facebook or Twitter can be an incredible sounding board for testing new musings and campaigns. You may get a comment or conversation moving, and you get fundamental info at the same time.

Conclusion

Congrats on enduring the section and through this book!

One of the most significant parts of online life advertising is guaranteeing your endeavors are effective in helping you meet your objectives.

To decide this, you'll have to monitor the entirety of your posts, on each channel. You can do this by evaluating and dealing with your web-based life measurements.

Social observation can be intriguing; I think an ideal approach to move toward it is to attempt a device like Hootsuite, use socialmention.com, and observe some Radian6 recordings. At that point, focus on growing great substance. When your social media nearness is going, I prescribe returning and utilizing the instruments.

Considering there are billions of individuals via web-based networking media today, it's anything but difficult to perceive any reason why such a significant number of organizations and advertisers utilize the channel to advance their items and draw in with clients.

Although deciding your organization's web-based life game-plan may appear to be overwhelming, you can abstain from feeling overpowered by understanding online life promoting patterns and utilizing a portion of the numerous assets accessible about the point. Along these lines, begin taking a shot at your business' online networking advertising methodology today to expand your number of adherents, improve commitment, and lift changes.

All the best!

Printed in Great Britain
by Amazon